HIT
GIRLS

HIT GIRLS

BRITNEY, TAYLOR, BEYONCÉ, AND THE WOMEN WHO BUILT POP'S SHINIEST DECADE

NORA PRINCIOTTI

BALLANTINE BOOKS
NEW YORK

Ballantine Books
An imprint of Random House
A division of Penguin Random House LLC
1745 Broadway, New York, NY 10019
randomhousebooks.com
penguinrandomhouse.com

Hardcover ISBN 978-0-593-72508-5
Ebook ISBN 978-0-593-72509-2

Printed in the United States of America on acid-free paper

1st Printing

FIRST EDITION

BOOK TEAM: Production editor: Andy Lefkowitz • Managing editor: Pamela Alders •
Production manager: Ali Wagner • Copy editor: Shasta Clinch •
Proofreaders: Dan Goff, Megha Jain, Karina Jha, and Lori Newhouse

Book design by Ralph Fowler

The authorized representative in the EU for product safety and compliance is
Penguin Random House Ireland, Morrison Chambers, 32 Nassau Street,
Dublin D02 YH68, Ireland. https://eu-contact.penguin.ie

For my parents

Contents

Introduction

It's the fall of 2003. I am nine years old, I have twenty dollars in my pocket, and I know exactly what I'm going to do with it. I've known for at least a week, ever since I won the money from my grandfather, his reward for the first time I swam to the dock in his local pond and back without stopping, but it's not until one of the first days of fourth grade when I'm afforded the chance to make my purchase. After school, I zip down to the library, where bookshelves have been pushed behind tables and covered up by cases displaying the bountiful offerings of the Scholastic Book Fair. I spy my target: a teal, tie-dye rectangle I've seen on the Disney Channel. There is a blond woman with windswept hair on the cover. The CD is near the register and I buy it immediately, plus two sparkly gel pens and a pack of gum. That just about exhausts my swim winnings, so I head straight out without browsing. I'm eager to get home, anyway. I have just purchased my very first album. It is Hilary Duff's *Metamorphosis*. This is the first day of the rest of my life.

You may be wondering why I wasn't buying, you know, *books* at the Scholastic Book Fair. To which I say, get lost, nerd! The thing was, I had books. I had a school library and my public library and parents who read to me and with me, and of course I loved those things but also took them for granted. Albums wrapped in shiny plastic were a different story. My ten-year-old existence took place mostly in the small New Hampshire town where I lived and the small town across the river in Vermont where I went to elementary school. These places had a lot to offer in the way of fresh air, summer nights lit up by fireflies, and artisan pottery studios, but shopping, particularly of the variety where one would buy various plastic-wrapped trinkets of the moment? The mall was two hours away. A trip with my mom during the holidays was my main commercial opportunity per annum. Because of this, the book fair at the start of each school year represented a kind of mass consumerism I found exhilarating. So I bought the album, and I thanked the good people of Scholastic for their superb taste.

At that time, Hilary Duff was the single most important person in the world to me outside my immediate family. What a woman! She was the star of my favorite Disney show, *Lizzie McGuire*, and my favorite Disney movie, the correspondingly titled *Lizzie McGuire Movie*, in which she got to ride a Vespa around Italy, a thing that no real teenagers do but movie teenagers do all the time. Duff was aspirational but relatable, and she was also a real pioneer in the butterfly hair clip space. My favorite part of *Lizzie McGuire* was how the show used a cartoon Lizzie pop-up to represent her inner monologue as she navigated various junior high dilemmas, a feature that resonated with me as someone with a chatty internal voice myself, and I watched and rewatched Lizzie, Gordo, Ethan, and Miranda as many afternoons as I could through third grade. I was obsessed with the *Lizzie McGuire Movie* soundtrack once it came out, particularly Atomic Kitten's "The Tide Is High," which I had on a HitClips mini MP3 player that hung off my backpack at all times. With the movie in the rearview, Duff herself was setting out to be a pop star, which happened to be the *exact category* of public figure I was most interested in.

Technically, *Metamorphosis* was not actually Duff's first album as a recording artist. She did a Christmas album in 2002 called *Santa Claus Lane,* though that is perhaps best lost to history. She was clearly promising, based on her contributions to the *Lizzie McGuire Movie* soundtrack, the songs "Why Not" and "What Dreams Are Made Of," which were, of course, iconic. But *Metamorphosis* was supposed to set Duff up for success as herself, not as Lizzie, and Hollywood Records, Disney's music label, shelled out for a dream team to make that happen. *Metamorphosis* was produced largely by the Matrix, a three-person team who'd blown up the year before for writing Avril Lavigne's "Complicated." Also in the room was John Shanks, a longtime touring guitarist in Melissa Etheridge's band who was just hitting it big as a songwriter and producer. In 2001, Shanks cowrote and produced several songs on Michelle Branch's breakout record, *The Spirit Room*, including its immaculately hooky lead single, "Everywhere," which became a Rosetta stone for the kind of guitar-driven pop sound Duff, like Lavigne and many others, was going for. Shanks's frequent writing partner, Kara DioGuardi (if you know the Cobra Starship featuring Leighton Meester collab "Good Girls Go Bad," and I think you do, you know her work), provided Duff with several tracks, including "Come Clean," which became the hit of the record.

I knew none of this at the time, of course, and I can't really say in hindsight that I should have, since I was ten and ten-year-olds don't really care about songwriting and production credits or the major-label hitmaking system. But on some level, I do think I understood that *Metamorphosis* was operating a cut above the average Radio Disney output, because I wore that album *out*. Sure, I was in the demographic sweet spot for lighthearted songs about youthful feelings over crunchy guitars, but that record is just plain good—it remains my personal opinion that any living being who doesn't feel something on the third chorus of "Come Clean" when Hilary hits the high note should be evaluated for sociopathic tendencies. I was not, and am not, alone in my appreciation—*Metamorphosis* was the eighth bestselling album of 2003, went triple platinum, and, over time, revealed itself as having a significant imprint on what I'd call the young millennial cultural canon. Duff's success paved the way for Disney crossover stars like Demi Lovato, the Jonas Brothers, and Miley Cyrus, and "Come Clean" found a lasting home over the opening credits to *Laguna Beach,* the pioneering MTV reality show that spun off into *The Hills,* and, eventually, most of our current rich-people-at-home genre of reality television. Over time, I've come to discover that *Metamorphosis* was many of my peers' first album as well, and I'm grateful both for that shared experience and for such an excellent gateway to the zeitgeist.

And what a zeitgeist it was. *Metamorphosis* brought me into the vibrant and rapidly mutating world of pop music in the early days of the 2000s. Britney. Christina. Avril. Bubblegum pop princesses and Warped Tour punks. Beyoncé in Destiny's Child and *Beyoncé* Beyoncé. Nelly *and* Nelly Furtado—the two most important Nellys! I know everyone thinks the music they grew up on is special, but I don't know of any other eras with a Kelly Clarkson! It was against this early-aughts backdrop that I became obsessed with pop culture and especially pop music. I became a passionate curator of mix CDs, which were labeled in Sharpie and stowed in a case that lived with my Walkman in the middle pocket of my JanSport backpack. I got into Pink and Ciara and Usher, and, eventually, a young artist by the name of Taylor Swift. In the evenings after school, I'd rush through my homework so that I could trawl Myspace and LimeWire pages for new songs and artists, or listen to ten-second previews on the brand-new iTunes store for anything catchy enough to add to my next mix. And for two forty-five-minute bus rides each school day, it was just me and my headphones.

Critically, I kept this burgeoning passion mostly to myself. An album like *Metamorphosis* was designed to be family friendly, something parents would happily buy for their kids and put on in the car. There's not an explicit song in Hilary Duff's entire discography. DioGuardi, the songwriter, had originally written "Come Clean" for herself, but when the song went to Duff, she changed the lyrics *let the rain come down and wet my dreams* to *and wake my dreams* so that it could stay mouse and parent approved. In my case, though, these efforts were unfortunately in vain. It's not that my parents were strict. They probably would have let me listen to Black Sabbath in the car if I'd been really into it. But at the time, the idea of letting them in on a piece of culture that resonated with me felt roughly as appealing as a root canal. This was obviously silly and a little comical—I remember a car ride to my grandparents' house with my mom a few summers after *Metamorphosis* was released where I attempted to watch the entirety of *Legally Blonde* in the back seat on her orange iBook laptop with my ear to the speakers in order to keep the volume low enough so that only I could hear it. This ended in disaster; my mom had a window cracked for most of the drive, but she happened to close it during the scene when the falsely accused Brooke Taylor Windham is convincing her legal team that she really did love her late husband despite their thirty-four-year age difference. By closing the window, the car got quiet just in time for my mom to hear Ali Larter suggest to her council that they show the jury "a picture of his dick" to prove she wasn't in it for the money. I had no idea what that meant, but I knew by my mom's reaction that it meant *something*, and obviously this whole experience was scarring enough that I'm telling you about it now.

I wasn't much more open with my peers, either. I was just shy, or, at least, someone who hadn't figured out how to let the more extroverted parts of my personality into the world. I had an easier time talking to teachers and my parents' friends than I did to my classmates for most of middle school. I should say, because I think my mom would want me to: I had wonderful friends! But I gatekept a lot of my likes and dislikes for fear of rejection. At my first slumber party, a cool girl named Katherine pulled a copy of *Tiger Beat* out from her pillowcase and suggested we all go around and say who was cuter, Orlando Bloom or Johnny Depp. I ended up being the only girl to say Orlando Bloom, which was of course a calamity of epic proportions and an incident that probably had an outsized impact on my general vibe during those years. Though I must say, the take holds up! Anyway, I mostly listened to my music on the bus or alone in my very teal bedroom.

If I am going to be sharing traumatic teen mag–related incidents from my youth, I should probably introduce myself. (In *Gossip Girl* voice.) And who am I? I'm Nora, nice to meet you! I'm an author and a podcast host, and in a perhaps predictable twist of making up for lost time, I've made a career out of writing and talking about my favorite slices of pop culture in music, sports, and TV. I am what you would call a "pop culture junkie," which makes me gag a little but is undeniably true, and basically just means that at any given moment I am liable to be thinking about Laura Dern. I also carry the groundbreaking distinction of being a millennial woman who loves Taylor Swift, whose discography I have covered extensively and adoringly on my podcast *Every Single Album.* And while I love movies and TV and fashion and awards shows and am fascinated by basically all elements of celebrity culture, as you may have guessed by now, there is a special place in my heart for the pop stars.

Clearly, I have come a long way in sharing this affinity. One could even make the argument I have overcorrected! From roughly 2017 to 2020, during which time I was a fully self-sufficient working adult, I kept a three-thousand-word document in my Notes app about Swift's career trajectory that I regularly shared with random acquaintances and captive-audience Hinge dates. There are men walking around the greater Boston area with this document on their phones right now, and I pray that none of them read this book and remember that is the case. That said, it's a joy to me that the music I love has become something I love to share. And while that says plenty about how I have grown since my preteen days, it also says something about how pop stardom itself has evolved.

Yes, the Bloom versus Depp incident may have loomed large, but I think the real reason I was afraid to display my love of pop music was that I had internalized the idea that it was considered stupid or girly—less cool than rock, or less significant than orchestral music. At least since the Beatles, young women have defined major trends in popular music, yet our tastes have often been trivialized. At the time of its coining in the early twentieth century, the phrase "pop music" was intended to denote a lite-listening quality more than it was meant to convey sheer popularity—the term was used to refer to music played on radio stations, as opposed to music that played in concert halls. Over time, it came to symbolize music that was either unserious, genreless, or seen as overtly commercial. An artist "going pop," for instance, often implies forsaking artistry or authenticity in the pursuit of sheer popularity. I grew up with two classical musicians as parents, so I definitely was exposed to the idea that there's Serious music and Unserious music. They did not do this on purpose—my mom and I wore out an ABBA greatest hits CD she kept in the car for many of my middle school years until it skipped so badly during "Dancing Queen" it had to be retired—but I understood the symbolism of things like dressing up to go to Symphony Hall versus listening to Britney Spears in my pajamas.

Through talking to friends and music fans over the years, I've come to understand that a lot of my peers picked up similar signals about their favorite pop stars and songs. Pop is a youthful genre, but the language used to describe it is often condescending, if not downright infantilizing. Fans are "teenyboppers," artists "pop princesses," and the music itself a "guilty pleasure." This has been the case since the earliest days of the recorded music industry—Frank Sinatra's young female fans in the 1940s were termed "bobby soxers," a "teenybopper" prevariant—but we early-aughts pop fans in particular were taught to understand our tastes in the especially muscular shadow of rock 'n' roll.

By our time, rock had been building the modern music industry in its image since the 1960s. The Rock & Roll Hall of Fame, for instance, is where we enshrine our most famous musicians; publications like *Rolling Stone,* a rock magazine, are home to much of the best writing about music in general. Pop needed rock to clearly define itself for the first time; for most of the twentieth century, the term hewed closer to that catchall definition of lite-listening music that played on the radio than a genre with any specific aesthetic principles. In the late 1970s and 1980s, though, a more specific idea of pop music and pop stardom coalesced around artists like Madonna and Michael Jackson, whose music built off new wave and disco scenes that were viewed as rock 'n' roll's opposition party. Their image of pop stardom, one of broad popularity, upbeat music, and an emphasis on spectacle proved sticky. Their music helped define pop as something closer to an actual genre than a radio format, and it's probably no accident that those lines became cleaner to draw once it was clear what *wasn't* within them, which was rock.

The disco-era definition of pop stardom was influential, but it was also narrow. Cross-pollination with other genres, especially, was limited. And before those divas had a chance to broaden our collective understanding of pop stardom into something more than a fad, the nineties came around, and the pop girls resumed occupying little sister status relative to the grunge and punk idols of the day and remained that way through the decade. Nineties rockers tended to be particularly disdainful of spotlights and spectacle, which meant that by the time Y2K came around, music coverage had a habit of deifying a certain set of aesthetic values that didn't align with pop music, casting the new wave of pop stars who broke out around that time in a particularly bubblegum-hued light. A *Rolling Stone* profile of *NSYNC from 2001, for instance, endorsed Justin Timberlake as helping then girlfriend Britney Spears "move from bubblegum to more rockish stuff," without questioning why that was a goal in the first place. Even as a kid, that implicit messaging was easy to intuit: Pop music was empty, corporate, and juvenile, and anyone with something real to say would quickly move beyond it if they hadn't ignored it in the first place. The prevalence of that kind of messaging meant it was easy to internalize, and if I'm not the only one it left with a slight persecution complex at the sight of a man carrying a Stratocaster, well, at least we came by it honestly.

Since then, I've gotten better about identifying and questioning these kinds of biases. But the perception of pop music and pop stars has also changed significantly. We take pop stars fairly seriously these days. We're not surprised when they win Grammys and we close read their lyrics like they're paragraphs of Camus. The average fan can rattle off the names of producers and data from the *Billboard* charts like an industry pro, and it's even common to describe groups of organized fans online in the terminology of war. We assume pop stars have a role to play in politics; some among us occasionally even accuse them of being Pentagon psyops! In 2023, two pop stars—Taylor Swift and Beyoncé—released concert films in theaters that revealed them as bigger box office draws than most movie stars. The tours featured in those movies were record-setting extravaganzas themselves—there was a while that summer when, if you read the news, you came away with the impression that the global economy was largely dependent on friendship bracelet supplies.

In the media, there's no shortage of thoughtful critical attention paid to the music of artists like Swift and Beyoncé, but also of Dua Lipa, Billie Eilish, Sabrina Carpenter, Olivia Rodrigo, Ariana Grande, Kacey Musgraves, Chappell Roan, and Charli XCX. In the general cultural discourse, the role of pop star is assumed to be filled by artists with skill and authorial intent, not by empty vessels for hooks, and the music made by pop stars can play with a wide range of musical styles from hip-hop to electronic music to country to, yes, rock 'n' roll.

The pop stars of the 2000s did not inherit this world, rather they invented it. In a decade of immense change—from how the music business transitioned from CDs to digital downloads and eventually to streaming, to how culture changed through an economic recession and a historic presidential election—these women redefined modern pop stardom, transforming an oft-trivialized role into a pop-cultural main character in a few key ways. By confronting old assumptions about genre, challenging the perception of celebrity and utilizing new technologies and the burgeoning internet to its fullest, the women of this era expanded our understanding of what a pop star could be and forced the industry around them to take them seriously. Rarely did these women reap the benefits of these changes in real time, but to understand how they made them happen, we have to go back in time—back to the start of a new decade in the halcyon days of the Slinky and the flip phone.

Each chapter in this book tells a story about a defining pop star of the aughts, or in some cases a group of them who fit together. Each of these stories will show their imprint on pop stardom. We'll cover how Britney Spears shocked adults into caring about pop, how Avril Lavigne confronted the idea of "selling out," how Kelly Clarkson represented the collapsing space between pop and indie, and how Taylor Swift harnessed the power of young women on the internet to create the world's most powerful fan base. I hope in the process of telling these stories, we'll afford these women the same kind of critical thought and appreciation they won for their contemporaries, but did not always get while the glossies and the tabloids and even the music press were more fixated on boyfriends and scandals. (The commodification of female celebrities' romantic lives is mostly grotesque, but, it must be said, too many of these women dated Wilmer Valderrama to avoid comment.) I also hope we'll reminisce and have some fun as we journey through the soundtrack of the aughts, a decade in pop music history that was chaotic and iconic in equal measure. I hope we will also recall some *really* ugly jeans.

A few notes before we begin! First, the stories I'm telling in this book are ones I think are necessary inclusions in any detailing of the pop history of the first decade of the 2000s. But they're also the ones I love, about the artists I love, a subjective account strongly influenced by the tastes of a somewhat dramatic preteen. To that end, I have taken a definite *okay now ladies!!!* approach—the stories in this book are women's stories. Being a pop star is not synonymous with being female (though the artists and audiences do skew in that direction) and there were major male artists like Usher, Justin Timberlake, and Maroon 5 who were absolutely pop stars. The early 2000s were, however, a particularly productive time for female artists. The aughts remain the only decade in music history where women made up more than half of the top twenty-five grossing artists in the United States. And thanks to the era's pronounced misogyny, it was also these women who were primarily placed in the most restrictive boxes of pop stardom—and who ultimately did the bulk of the work to break them down. Also, I can't write about Maroon 5 because then I'd have to tell you that my first crush was Adam Levine.

A second thing I'd like to lay out is my working definition of "pop star." While "pop music" no longer refers simply to music played outside of concert halls, it's inherently slippery to define a genre based on the moving target of what's popular. My definition of pop has to do with its mass appeal and how it's made, largely inside a major-label system full of super producers, audience-testers, and star-chasers undergoing the glorious, ridiculous, messy work of making music that captures our collective attention. It's more value set than specific sound—pop is big and bright and spectacular, it's of the moment, it's unashamed of appealing to masses or putting on a show. I will also sometimes refer to "pure pop," which I associate more closely with a specific musical aesthetic: steady, up-tempo beats, a devotion to the hook, synthesizers, and the general desire to be as much like Madonna as possible. Being a pop star also does not preclude being a star in another genre, and I'll identify those dualities when they occur as well.

Third, though "the 2000s" can be used to refer to the entire twenty-first century, I will be using it to refer to the first decade of that century alone, if only so I can avoid using "the aughts" on every reference. If I mean the entire twenty-first century I will refer to it that way.

The final bit of context I want to cover is the relationship between pop, hip-hop, and R&B. The surge of rap and hip-hop in the nineties, aughts, and onward was at least as important in shifting the center of the musical mainstream as anything that has happened in "pure" pop, and you will hear a statistically reasoned argument within for why it was probably more important. You cannot write about how music changed in the 2000s without considering artists like Missy Elliott, Jay-Z, Kanye West, Rihanna, Beyoncé, Lil Jon, Ciara, Usher, and T-Pain, who had roots in hip-hop, R&B, and dancehall but who were also an inarguable part of the pop ecosystem, just as artists like Spears interacted significantly with R&B. Pop won respect not by replacing rock 'n' roll as the music industry's supreme genre, but by thriving during a time that awarded genre flexibility and ultimately led to a reduced importance of genre overall. There's plenty of room in pop for hip-hop hitmakers, as well as for reggae, disco, electronic music, and rock stars, but the labels matter a lot less than they did in the aughts because of changes that took place during the decade, not just in the pop ecosystem.

To these ends, pop and hip-hop often operated in tandem. You will see them overlap and interplay many times in this book, but know that I inevitably look through a pop-focused lens. A comprehensive look at how popular music changed our culture in the 2000s would be definitionally incomplete without a focus on the boundary-pushers in rap and hip-hop who were the most significant forces in crafting contemporary popular music. Those stories deserve their own book—I would be eager to read it—and some already exist, which I highly suggest you seek out. Steve Stoute's *The Tanning of America* examines how hip-hop altered culture and grew to span demographic barriers from a consumer marketing perspective. Kelefa Sanneh's *Major Labels* is a fantastic look at the history of genres in general and contains chapters on both hip-hop and pop.

This book, though, is concerned with my all-time faves. It's a love letter to those millennial middle school jams we're still scream-singing at wedding receptions. It is a chance to argue, once and for all, for Mandy Moore's significant place in history if only so I'll stop doing so at parties. It's a place to examine the half-dozen musical lives of Britney Spears and how Rihanna became the only billionaire anyone thinks is cool. We will be remembering some guys in this book. We will be talking about Myspace, Carson Daly, and Lindsay Lohan. I hope we'll uncover a few new stories about how the music of this era was made, and I hope we'll have fun reminiscing before we all get back to swapping tips for retinoid creams.

So let's go, shall we, on a journey through a musical decade with a group of artists who built my world, and quite a bit of ours. Oh, baby, baby . . .

HIT
GIRLS

1

How Britney Spears
Ended the Nineties

THE DAWN OF THE TWENTY-FIRST CENTURY WAS CHAR-acterized, primarily, by something that did not happen. I have some fuzzy recollections of Y2K, the panic at the end of the 1990s that ensued after a handful of computer scientists raised concerns that the new year would bring mass system failure and worldwide chaos since computer code, which categorized what year it was by the last two digits of the annum, would be unable to tell the difference between 1900 and 2000. As I write this, I have an espionage instrument of the Chinese military in my pocket that I use to watch cat videos and Jeff Bezos controls my supply of toilet paper, so all the fuss seems kind of quaint, but I am told it was a Whole Big Deal. In 1999, *Time* magazine ran an issue with the words "The End of the World!?!" on its cover. But then, Y2K arrived with little incident. The lights stayed on. Trains ran on time. Society remained intact.

Which . . . obviously. The changing of a clock does not define a new era. Only Britney Spears can do that.

On September 29, 1998, Jive Records released Britney Spears's single ". . . Baby One More Time" to contemporary hits radio stations across the United States. Though the calendar wouldn't flip centuries for another fifteen months, the moment those glottal *oh baby, baby*s hit the airwaves was the moment that the aughts began in pop culture and in music. But ". . . Baby One More Time" and the birth of Britney as the defining pop star of the 2000s was more than just a kickoff event. Before the aughts could become a period in which pop stardom changed, they had to become an especially fertile one for pop music in the first place, and it was Britney Spears who made sure they did. By creating an indelible pop classic, clearing Max Martin's path to become the defining producer of the decade, and by using provocation to reach older and broader audiences than the teen pop of the late 1990s, Spears paved the way for pop music to flourish in the early 2000s.

Let's set the stage a bit. The day before ". . . Baby One More Time" debuted, Aerosmith's "I Don't Want to Miss a Thing" was the number-one song on the *Billboard* Hot 100 and had been for a month. Filling out most of the lower rungs of the chart was a mix of radio-friendly country (Shania Twain, LeAnn Rimes, Faith Hill), hip-hop and R&B (Usher, Brandy, Puff Daddy), and a smattering of Third Eye Blind–variant rock bands.

Radio had been in a bit of a bind. Grunge had dominated the midnineties, and while Radiohead, Nirvana, the Red Hot Chili Peppers, and Pearl Jam were the biggest bands in the world to the MTV audience, their themes of alienation and dejection weren't great mainstream radio fodder. Nirvana front man Kurt Cobain's death by suicide in 1994 had been a turning point for artists, too—the genre lost its chief spokesperson, and the disaffection of its other leading men became harder to venerate when it had such fatal consequences. Grunge morphed either into nu metal, which made even less sense on Top 40 radio, which on a national level was becoming increasingly homogenized thanks to conglomerate station ownership, or softer alt-rock, which was more palatable but less interesting. Few DJs felt like they were on the cutting edge spinning Sugar Ray during drive time, and audiences were dwindling. In 1996 alone, New York contemporary hits station Z100 lost a third of its audience. The station fell into eighteenth place, in large part by leaning heavily into a waning alt-rock scene. A shake-up followed, and several new executives, including a young programmer named Sharon Dastur, were brought in to right the ship. On her first day, Dastur walked into the station and was surprised to find Alice in Chains playing on the morning show and Soundgarden signed up for another guest slot. "I'm like, 'What is this? This is not Top 40,'" Dastur told me.

There's an idea in radio about how the types of sounds that are popular in music ebb and flow, particularly as it pertains to Top 40. It comes from a man named Guy Zapoleon, a fifty-year veteran of the radio industry and longtime Top 40 program director who now consults for stations. In 1992, Zapoleon published an argument that, since 1956, the modern era of popular recorded music could be explained as a cycle with three stages repeating itself roughly every ten years. Zapoleon argued that the cycle begins with a "pure pop" stage, where there's a supply of good pop music with mass appeal, as well as rock, hip-hop, and R&B that bleeds into pop. The pure pop stage is the best stage for a Top 40 radio programmer. The second stage that follows is what Zapoleon calls "the extremes," in which music moves toward its edges, usually alternative rock and hip-hop, looking for freshness and innovation that younger listeners enjoy but loses something in mass appeal. For a radio programmer, the challenge of "the extremes" is that a good amount of the most relevant music doesn't quite fit on Top 40 radio. This leads to the third stage, "the doldrums," where pop is dull and overwrought, cut off from the edgier happenings in rock, R&B, and hip-hop, and flounders until there's something, or someone, fresh in pure pop to bring the cycle back around. And in the late nineties, pop radio was deep in the doldrums.

But cycles being cycles, a new one was around the bend. Zapoleon considers its starting point to be 1997 with the arrival of the teen pop wave and, specifically, the arrival of the Spice Girls in North America. The girl group had been initially shortchanged as a euro phenomenon that would never work in the United States, historically snobbier when it comes to bubblegum pop than European countries, but this proved incorrect quickly. Sporty, Ginger, Posh, Baby, and Scary had "Wannabe" at number one on the Hot 100 for four straight weeks in January 1997 and their debut album *Spice* sold at least twenty-three million copies.

It's hard to overstate the degree of international megastardom the Girls achieved, seemingly, overnight. The same year *Spice* hit America, the Girls visited South Africa for a charity concert and met Nelson Mandela, who called them his "heroines" and told reporters that meeting them was one of the greatest moments of his life. In an attempt at some good PR in the wake of the death of Princess Diana, then Prince Charles attended the concert and brought along a young Prince Harry, who was nursing a bit of a crush on Geri Halliwell, a.k.a. Ginger. It's a sadness to me that Peter Morgan's Netflix series *The Crown* never did anything with this material; reportedly, one Spice Girl grabbed Charles's butt during their meet and greet, and I can only imagine how Dominic West would have played that moment. Ultimately, Charles's attempt to seem like less of a fuddy-duddy backfired when the British press determined that Diana never would have made Harry wear a suit to a Spice Girls show, but the young prince did get to meet his fellow Ginger. Halliwell also had a notable moment in her closing remarks at the concert: "I think there's a classic speech that Nelson Mandela did, I can't remember exactly, but he mentioned never suppress yourself, never make yourself feel small for others' insecurities," she said. "And that's what girl power is all about." Hear, hear, Geri—no notes.

In the United States, the fact that audiences embraced *Spice* did seem to indicate that they were ready for a new pop movement. Two years earlier, in 1995, the producer Clive Calder and infamous boy band manager Lou Pearlman had tried to debut the Backstreet Boys with "We've Got It Goin' On." But while the song was a hit in Europe, it got no traction for the group on US airwaves. In June 1997 they tried again, releasing "Quit Playing Games (With My Heart)" as a single. This time, with more and more of the children of baby boomers coming of age every day, we were ready. By August, the song was at number two on the Hot 100. Suddenly, the Spice Girls, Backstreet Boys, *NSYNC, and Hanson all became household names in America, and their mix of new jack swing rhythms and orchestral hits with croon-worthy pop melodies was all over the radio and MTV. Teen pop was a sensation, and because it capitalized on the last days of the pre-Napster era when CDs were flying off shelves, it was also staggeringly lucrative. Backstreet nearly matched *Spice*'s sales numbers with twenty-five million copies sold, and every kid knew which Spice Girl or Backstreet Boy they identified with, crushed on, or both. But as long as its audience was concentrated within one generation's youth, it was destined to crest.

That crest was approaching quickly as Y2K neared. "Quit Playing Games" is still Backstreet's highest-charting song. The Spice Girls released only three studio albums. Neither they, Backstreet, or

*NSYNC would be together five years after *Spice* took over the world. Charges of juvenilia are often unfairly levied against pop acts, but it's fair to say the aesthetics of nineties teen pop were probably just a little too youthful for true lasting power. The fact that nineties teen pop was centered around boy bands and girl groups as opposed to solo acts, too, made individual members more anonymous—there were plenty of people who knew Backstreet, but didn't really know Howie or Brian. For pop to get the kind of traction in the new millennium that was impossible to dismiss as a teen fad, something or someone was going to have to synthesize that bright pop sound with a persona that was more interesting to older audiences. Someone a little less . . . innocent.

The first listeners to hear ". . . Baby One More Time" would have been forgiven for not recognizing that they were hearing the start of a new era when it hit their ears. They would have been forgiven for not understanding what they were hearing at all when they first heard its tangle of funk bass, panting percussion, and Spears's alien drawl—her accent seems to come from somewhere between Kentwood, Louisiana, where she grew up, and one of the bays of Mars. ". . . Baby One More Time" is one of those songs that almost anyone, even without trying, has heard so many times that it's near impossible to hear the song just as its component parts—the lyrics, the harmonies, the melody—it's just ". . . Baby One More Time." I've heard it in taxis, at bars, in a SoulCycle class, in my dermatologist's office, and once, notably, at 4:30 a.m. in a Delta Sky lounge that had no right to be going that hard at such an hour. But try to imagine that you're hearing the song fresh, without any expectations of where it's going, when the hook will come in, or who the singer is, and you'll realize how *strange* sounding it is, starting with Spears's downright bizarre treatment of the words she's singing. The word "know" winds up with two syllables, and when the vocal comes in, there are extra *a*s and *y*s all over the place. It's as if she took a look at the lyric sheet and thought, *I have better plans for these vowel sounds. I* before *E,* except if it's Britney, bitch, if you will.

The verse continues, its tango with English phonation interspersed with that baseline and the repeated three-chord hit that echoes the first thing you hear in the song, until Ms. Spears reaches the pre-chorus. Up until this point the song has been merely strange, but now it crosses over into nonsensical territory. To the extent there is a "plot" to ". . . Baby One More Time," it makes no sense. Britney wants the song's object to show her things and tell her things, implying that they're there with her, but also, she's lonely and they're not there with her.

Never mind the fact that she's the one who shouldn't have let them go. It gets a bit circular. But I don't ever remember getting hung up on this at the time this song entered my consciousness because before there is time to parse its internal logic or linguistic choices, the chorus has arrived, and nothing else matters. Her loneliness is killing her, but she still believes. So do you.

The chorus, of course, makes even less sense than the verse, which, of course, does not matter, either. It keeps coming back around, chords resolving, those three hits returning over and over again, propelling the song. Spears's vocal swells and brightens, a diva-lite belt replacing the tighter, percussive delivery on the first verse, then reverts to its old form, stranger and more staccato than before in time for the second. The single weirdest delivery in the entire song is on the word "breathe" in the line "the reason I breathe is you" in the second verse. Spears adds another full extra syllable to the end of the word, except it's just a whoosh of air. She pushes that sound out and then goes right back to her slithering vocal fry on the words "is you" like nothing ever happened. There's been far too much discourse over the years about most parts of Britney Spears's body, but not nearly enough about her epiglottis. By the end of the song, different versions of Spears singing are layered together, sometimes fighting, sometimes supporting each other until they all band together for one final request—to give her a sign, to hit her, baby, one more time.

The song ends on one last—one more—orchestral hit and just like that, nothing would ever be the same.

Spears got one more and then some: ". . . Baby One More Time" spent two weeks at number one on the *Billboard* Hot 100 and went on to sell over ten million copies, making it one of the bestselling singles of all time. In 2020, *Rolling Stone* named it the greatest debut single ever, with good reason—few songs can claim to have charted the course for an entire musical generation like ". . . Baby One More Time."

I'm pretty sure by this point, given her multi-decade career, the slew of documentaries recently devoted to reexamining her backstory, and her bestselling 2023 memoir *The Woman in Me,* you know who Britney Spears is and her whole *deal,* but some quick review just in case. There is a well-established and sometimes horrifyingly detailed record of Spears's early life in media accounts and that slew of documentaries, little of which Spears herself seems to appreciate, so I will keep this brief: Spears was born in 1981 in McComb, Mississippi, to mother Lynne and father Jamie Spears, who soon moved the family to Kentwood. Jamie was a construction worker whose struggles with alcohol destabilized the family, while Lynne ran a daycare center and was shuttling Britney to and from dance lessons and recitals by the time her daughter was four years old. Britney sought out structure and control in performance, from singing to dancing to gymnastics. Her primary passion was performing onstage, though, and she spent much of ages eight to fifteen trying to make it as a child star. One of her earliest jobs was as an understudy to Laura Bell Bundy in an off-Broadway musical called *Ruthless!*, which is about—I'm so serious—an ambitious child actor named Tina who murders her third-grade classmate so she can have the lead in the school play. In act II, Tina shoots her own mother, declares there's no money in theater, and moves to Hollywood to try to book a TV series. Before any of this happens, Tina delivers the best line of the show, telling her mother, "I've had a normal childhood. It's time to move on," which is some pretty wild foreshadowing if you ask me. Anyway, Britney never actually stayed with the gig long enough to see *Ruthless!* open. Spears wound up competing on the junior version of the TV singing competition *Star Search,* but after losing in the finals, she and Lynne decided to leave New York and go home, and Britney was replaced as Bell Bundy's understudy by another wannabe child actor by the name of Natalie Portman.

Eventually, Spears landed a role on Disney's *The Mickey Mouse Club,* alongside cast members including Justin Timberlake, Ryan Gosling, and Christina Aguilera—no one has been on a hotter streak than the *Mouse Club* casting department in the midnineties. Spears spent two years as a Mouseketeer until the show was canceled in 1996. After that, Britney went back to Louisiana and enrolled in junior high but kept looking for ways to open doors as a performer. Her family knew an entertainment lawyer named Larry Rudolph whose clients included the Backstreet Boys, Toni Braxton, and Lou Pearlman, the former manager of both Backstreet and *NSYNC who is infamous specifically for perpetrating the longest-running Ponzi scheme in United States history, and generally for being a blimp magnate from Orlando, Florida. (Pearlman, who also embezzled money from the bands he managed and trapped members in predatory contracts, was sentenced to twenty-five years in prison in 2008.) Anyway, Rudolph agreed to meet with Britney, and after sensing that she had *something*, signed her and agreed to help her get a record deal, at which point it was time for Britney and those now guiding her hopeful career to decide what kind of songs she wanted to sing.

On *Star Search,* Spears had performed "I Don't Care," a vaudeville tune originally performed by Eva Tanguay, and "Love Can Build A Bridge," by female country duo the Judds, which she'd also sung at an aunt's wedding. She was a belter, with a Broadway-esque delivery, leaning on the lowest part of her register. (There is a splash of Lea Michele as Rachel Berry as Fanny Brice going on in the performance!) She kept a definite showbiz streak, but by the time she was post-*Mouse,* Britney was also into R&B, especially Janet Jackson, Whitney Houston, and Mariah Carey. When Rudolph needed a song for Britney to record as a demo, he chose one that had been intended for Braxton, another soft R&B belter. The song had been rejected by Braxton for sounding too young, but when Rudolph told Spears to put herself on tape singing it, he suggested she listen to Braxton's recording of it and emulate it as closely as possible. When that tape garnered auditions for Britney for three labels— Epic, Mercury, and Jive—she and Rudolph chose Houston's "I Will Always Love You" and "I Have Nothing" for her a cappella performances in front of A&R executives in their various Manhattan offices. Epic and Mercury both passed. For the 2010 biography *Britney: Inside the Dream,* Epic's vice president of A&R, Michael Caplan, told author Steve Dennis that he was unimpressed by her voice, seemingly holding the fifteen-year-old up against the woman whose song she was singing.

"I was expecting a true artiste and in walked a shy little girl," Caplan said.

This was obviously not Caplan's finest moment of A&Ring, missing Spears's massive capacity for artistry and generally sounding like a bit of a snob. But in dismissing Britney as not-Whitney, he had actually identified a piece of what needed to click into place in order for a clear vision of Spears as a pop singer to come together. According to John Seabrook, author of *The Song Machine: Inside the Hit Factory,* Jive A&R man Steve Lunt didn't like Spears's belting diva vocals either. "Britney was trying to sing like Toni Braxton [on her demo], which was way too low for her. It sounded pretty awful in places," Lunt said. "But when her voice went up high, you could hear the girlish quality, and there was something really appealing about that." Lunt had identified one of Spears's key traits— her dueling senses of both innocence and maturity—which belting out ballads didn't tap into. With the blessing of label head Clive Calder, Jive offered Spears a ninety-day contract that the label could extend in the event they liked where things were headed.

Though Jive had not made a long-term commitment to Spears yet, it was clear that the vision for her was to do teen pop. Spears had maintained her interest in country from her *Star Search* days and said she saw herself doing "Sheryl Crow music, but younger," but the label saw her as a pop star. Jive's roster of artists was concentrated around rappers, R&B singers, and boy bands, and Calder felt there was an open lane for a female solo artist. Most of the acts pushing that wave were boy bands like *NSYNC, the Backstreet Boys, Five, or Hanson, girl groups like the Spice Girls, Destiny's Child, or B*Witched (there will be no "C'est la Vie" erasure in this book!), or mixed-gender groups like S Club 7. Calder felt that the best blueprint for Spears to follow was Robyn, the brilliant Swedish pop singer who would soon post back-to-back top-ten hits in the United States in 1997 with "Do You Know (What It Takes)" and "Show Me Love." Britney might have had other ideas before, but she got it instinctively and accepted that teen pop made sense for a simple reason: "Because I can dance to it—it's more me."

Dancing was important. Spears might have imagined herself as a folksy Sheryl Crow type, but she had an instinct for spectacle. Lunt, who (along with Eric Foster White, the lone pop producer at Zomba, Jive's publishing imprint) had been assigned to shepherd her musical direction, told Seabrook that he learned this when he showed Britney Robyn's video for "Show Me Love," in which Robyn, wearing long black pants and a black long-sleeved shirt with a collar, walks through a crowd of young people doing activities like making out, dribbling a basketball, and playing a keyboard bass. "She said, 'The record is really good, but the video is all wrong. It's in boring black and white and no one is dancing. If it was me I'd be wearing a miniskirt and I'd be dancing,'" Lunt said. Miniskirts were important, too.

On the strength of some okay original songs ("From the Bottom of My Broken Heart," which would make Spears's first album, is one) recorded with Lunt and White and a cover of the Jets' "You Got It All" that sold Calder, Jive picked up the option on Spears. Everyone agreed that Robyn, plus dancing, plus miniskirts was the way to go. In turn, that meant Sweden was the way to go. In particular, one Swede: Max Martin.

Max Martin, born Karl Martin Sandberg, was a Stockholm-based producer with long shaggy hair who'd been tutored under another Stockholm-based producer with long shaggy hair named Denniz Pop. Denniz was a former DJ with a knack for coming up with melodies, and he'd become a successful producer by turning dance tracks into radio-friendly hits. Denniz essentially got his big break by accident—in 1992, the Swedish pop group Ace of Base sent him a demo of their song "All That She Wants," which he ignored until the tape got stuck in his car stereo. Forced to listen to the demo over and over for a period of two weeks, Denniz eventually started hearing a way to rearrange the tune so that the catchiest part—a whistled melody that, on the demo, came at the end—could become the intro to the song. He added a kick drum and a baseline, and he had a hit. "All That She Wants" became the first number-one hit from Sweden in the UK since ABBA and went to number one in the US on the *Billboard* Hot 100.

That same year, in 1992, Denniz founded Cheiron Studios and began collecting a stable of producer protégés. One of those pupils was Sandberg, a French-horn-student-turned-glam-metal-enthusiast whose deepest, darkest secret was that he was an absolute sucker for pop, something he never shared with his fellow metalheads. Sandberg quickly became indispensable to Denniz—not just because they shared a knack for composing catchy melodies but because he could read music well and was trained in music theory, which Denniz, taught only by his gut instinct, was not. They were a great pair. In 1995, the two released their first coproduction, the single "Right Type of Mood" off Herbie Crichlow's album *Fingers,* though not before Denniz decided that his partner needed a more compelling disco name than Karl Sandberg for the production credit. "I arrived at the studio one day," Sandberg said in a 2008 Radio Sweden documentary, *The Cheiron Saga,* "and the single had just been cut and I was looking at it, and it was such an amazing experience to be holding it. It read 'Produced by Denniz Pop and Max Martin.'"

"Hmm. Who's that?" Sandberg asked.

To which everyone else in the room responded, "It's *you!*"

"Oh, okay," Sandberg said. "And that was my name from that point on."

By 1998, Martin was the go-to producer for teen pop. Alongside Denniz, he'd churned out hits for the Backstreet Boys, *NSYNC, and Robyn, which had established Cheiron's signature sound. Fundamentally, that sound was a combination of ABBA-esque euro pop chords, big eighties rock choruses, and grooves at least vaguely reminiscent of the new jack swing movement in American R&B put through a European filter. The special sauce was Martin's supernatural gift for melody and zealous allegiance to a principle he calls "melodic math."

The idea behind the melodic math principle is that every part of a song should be in service of the melody, which is the first thing he writes. The lyrics, and the vocal delivery of those lyrics, for example, exist to support those melodies, with most syllables neatly assigned to one particular note in a melody. If you want to hear melodic math in action, one good song to turn on is Katy Perry's "Teenage Dream." Queue it up and listen to how neatly the syllables are tied to notes in the melody: Each word of the line *you make me* and each syllable of the words "teenage dream" emphasizes a single note in the melody of the chorus. The words exist in order to get the sounds to sink in, part of why Martin's songs are often such earworms. And Martin is dogmatic about his own rules. Let's say a lyric is poetic but doesn't naturally end at the end of a melodic phrase. With Martin, it's the lyric that has to change to fit, not the melody, even if the poeticism is diminished by changing the words or the scan. Which is how you get *I never wanna hear you say I want it that way.*

It makes no sense, given that the boys are asking the song's object to explain their own thoughts to them, but also to never speak, but also to tell them *why* over and over again. Things get even more jumbled when one factors in the verses, where Nick Carter has already told the object of the song to believe *him* when he says that *he* wants it that way, whatever way that is and whomever is supposed to be, or supposed to *not* be, requesting that things be as such. Men would rather never want to hear you say you want it that way than go to therapy, etc. etc.

The A&R team at Jive Records actually tried to intervene and change the lyrics to the song before it was released in 1999 as the lead single for the Backstreet Boys' third studio album, the thirteen-times platinum-certified *Millennium*. They wanted to get rid of all the "tell me whys" with lines like "no goodbyes" and "no more lies." They were logically a lot more sound than the original, but also somehow much worse. Maybe there's a weightlessness to a message you can't quite comprehend that makes the song the confection it is—the "that's that me espresso" school of hitmaking, if you will. Maybe the word "I" takes too much emphasis in the second-to-last line relative to the second syllable of "wanna" and it makes the melodic math feel unsolved. In any case, the boys stuck with Martin's version, and it worked out pretty well.

Melodic math aside, another reason Martin's songs contain lyrics that sound a bit off is that he's a Swede writing in a second language. Going all the way back to ABBA, one factor in the international success of Swedish pop musicians has been the fact that Sweden imports a lot of English-speaking movies, books, television, and other media and entertainment products—studies have found that even a third of TV commercials aired in Sweden contain English—but it's understandable that idioms and certain phrases were bound to get lost in translation. "I grew up on Elton John and the Beatles and I had no idea what they were saying, it was just gibberish," Martin told *The Telegraph* in 2019. "If we come to a place in a writing session where one word might be better sense [*sic*] but the other option sounds cool, I will always pick the one that sounds appealing to me." When it comes to the least comprehensible Cheiron lyrics to make it to air, "I Want It That Way" doesn't even crack my personal top five:

5. *Sadness is beautiful / Loneliness is tragical*—Backstreet Boys, "Shape of My Heart." Of *course* they stuck AJ with "tragical." Martin produced this song with Rami Yacoub, a

Cheironite who was his right-hand man during the Britney and Backstreet years and who went on to produce many of One Direction's greatest hits. (Rami crushed the beats on Backstreet's *Black & Blue* album, especially "The Call.") "Shape of My Heart" is, for my money, the best Backstreet song even though it takes a very non-Cheiron-like forty full seconds to get going. There is no juicier melody in the catalog, "I Want It That Way" included, and I swear this is true. Still . . . *tragical.*

4. *Tell me, I'm not in the blue*—Britney Spears, "(You Drive Me) Crazy." Best guess, the Cheiron boys mixed up "out of the blue" and "in the dark" to get this one. Idioms were not their strong suit. The electric guitar shredding at the end of the original version of the song? Very much their strong suit.

3. *All that she wants / is another baby*—Ace of Base, "All That She Wants." The earliest and one of the best Cheironisms— I suppose we should cut them some slack here given that *no one* involved in making the song was a native English speaker. (Jonas, Linn, and Jenny Berggren and Ulf Ekberg, the bandmembers, were all native Swedes, which is how they knew of Denniz Pop so early on.)

Credit their global sensibilities for knowing that the reggae-lite baseline of "All That She Wants" would click in a New York club setting, or that the chorus's melody, set over chords, would be fun to sing while speeding down the Pacific Coast Highway. Those sensibilities did not extend, however, to understanding that the lyrics sound like they refer to a woman who desperately wants a child, not a boyfriend.

2. *I only wanna die alive / Never by the hands of a broken heart*—Ariana Grande featuring Zedd, "Break Free." First of all, some of you may at this point be going, *he wrote that song too?!* Yes, and he's not slowing down. If this list was intended to show the breadth of Martin's discography, I'd have included *I can't feel my face when I'm with you / but I love it,* from the Weeknd's "Can't Feel My Face," but I am told that if you do a lot of cocaine that actually scans. Anyway, in 2014, while recording the song for Grande's album *My Everything,* Martin had to convince her to sing the lyrics as they were despite her reluctance toward the idea of dying alive and making the incorrect assertion that hearts have hands. "I fought him on it the whole time," Grande said. " 'I am not going to sing a grammatically incorrect lyric, help me God!' Max was like, 'It's funny—just do it!' I know it's funny and silly but grammatically incorrect things make me cringe sometimes." Martin and his melodic math won out, though, which perhaps had something to do with the fact that he had seventeen number-one hits to his name by that point. The line stayed.

Which brings us to number one, and back to . . . *Hit me baby one more time.*

Martin did not write ". . . Baby One More Time" with Spears in mind. He felt it was a song for a group and had initially offered it to the Backstreet Boys and TLC, both of which passed on it because of the lyrics. "I was like, I like the song but do I think it's a hit? Do I think it's TLC? I'm not saying 'hit me baby,' " Tionne "T-Boz" Watkins later told MTV's Cory Midgarden, recalling the decision not to record the song. The heart of the issue was a misunderstanding of slang. The phrase Martin and his Scandi cohorts were searching for was "hit me up." They believed that "hit me baby" conveyed a request to call someone back (sort of like when my mom asks if I'm going to "hook up" with one of my friends later). To T-Boz, it sounded strange at best and like an allusion to domestic violence at worst. Besides, Martin was coming up against another one of his cultural limitations. The vast majority of Swedish people are white, and its national history is not so inexorably interwoven with racial baggage as, say, American history. This has often been an advantage: One of Martin's gifts has always been the ability to weave R&B grooves into pop songs in ways that American producers might (perhaps rightly) believe to be appropriative or outside of their range. But it also means that his radar for certain cultural shibboleths in how a song sounds isn't always sharp. Martin heard ". . . Baby One More Time" as an R&B song, with its slap bass and hip-hop cliché orchestral hits, but to ears that had spent more time outside of Stockholm, the Cheiron version of those sounds did not sound authentic. "All those chords are so European; how could that possibly be an American R&B song? No Black artist was going to sing it," Lunt said. "But that was the genius of Max Martin. Without being fully aware of it, he'd forged a brilliant sound all his own."

Max offered the song to Robyn next, but she didn't wind up recording it, either. Jive, which had a relationship with Martin from hiring him to work with Backstreet, had asked him to write some songs for Spears, so he figured he might rework the demo and see if they'd like it for her. He did, finishing the hooks with his own vocals, filling in what would be verses with open vowel sounds and leaving the bridge for later—if his audience wasn't sold by the first chorus there was no point to the song, anyway—and mailed it to New York. Lunt recalled the reception to the demo in Jive's offices this way: "Holy shit, this is perfect."

Like they did when she watched the Robyn video and called for more miniskirts and dancing, Spears's instincts kicked in when she heard ". . . Baby One More Time." She got the song immediately. Instead of being a turnoff, its taboo quality appealed to her taste for spectacle—the dash of discomfort was what made the song memorable. She heard it not just as flirty, but a little desperate, which played into the ambiguousness of "hit me." (As a means of papering over the issue, the label changed the title of the song, which Martin had been calling "Hit Me Baby (One More Time)" to ". . . Baby One More Time," but even there, the ellipsis reads like a wink.) The night before Spears recorded the vocals for ". . . Baby," she stayed up all night to make her voice sound extra raspy; later that year she told *Rolling Stone* that she spent those long waking hours listening to Soft Cell's "Tainted Love" over and over again, thinking about channeling Marc Almond's pleading yelp into her vocal. "What a sexy song," she said. Though it was her girlish upper register that got Jive to sign her, it's Spears's low voice that puts ". . . Baby One More Time" in its alluring purr. "I wanted my voice to just be able to groove with the track. So the night before, I stayed up really, really late, so when I went into the studio, I wasn't rested. When I sang it, I was just laid-back and mellow—it sounds cool, though. You know how it sounds really low in the lower register—it sounds really sexy." The results would define the first era of pop music in the 2000s, send every major label searching for more new pop talent, and provide Martin with his first number-one hit.

". . . Baby" performed well in the first month after its release. Spears went around the country, performing the song in shopping malls to increasingly large crowds looking up from their Panda Express or taking a break from browsing at Claire's. On November 21, ". . . Baby One More Time" made the *Billboard* Hot 100 chart for the first time, slotting in healthily at number seventeen. Five days after that was when the dam broke. The song's music video premiered on MTV.

The ". . . Baby One More Time" music video was where Spears, sixteen at the time, fully articulated the combination of girlish pep and adult provocation that separated her from her teen pop predecessors and made her *the* cultural obsession of the early aughts. In the video, Spears, playing a bored girl at school, waits for the bell to ring at the end of class, then struts through the hallways as the leader of a dance parade. Her shirt is knotted above her belly button and her hair is in braids fixed with puffy pink bows; the aesthetic signals of youthfulness and sex appeal are decidedly mixed.

Notably, this approach was Spears's idea. Nigel Dick, who directed the ". . . Baby" video, originally conceived it as a cartoon superhero story with a Power Rangers aesthetic. That video would have been much more in line with standard kid fare, and less provocative, but Spears nixed it immediately. She wasn't interested in Power Rangers. She wanted to channel what was cool to her as a sixteen-year-old girl, which is to say that she wanted to be at school with friends, thinking about boys, with miniskirts and dancing. She said as much on set. Spears would later tell *People* that she was responsible for the bare midriffs, too. "The outfits looked kind of dorky, so I was like, 'Let's tie up our shirts and be cute,'" she said. To her, it was perfectly age appropriate. Every girl in the United States was wearing Soffe shorts with the waistband rolled over to show more skin; why couldn't she tie up her shirt over a sports bra, showing nothing more than she would have in a dance class after school? Some of the producers were skeptical about the coquettish look and thought she should cover up, but Britney got her way. Dick gave his okay, and the video was shot in three days at Venice High School, also the shooting location for the high school scenes in *Grease*.

The video took off. Its release came just two months after the first episode of *Total Request Live* aired on MTV, in an era in which a great music video could sell a song, a look, or a whole career. Off that success, every part of Spears's rollout campaign went into overdrive. . . . *Baby One More Time* the album was released on January 12, 1999, and on February 9, ". . . Baby One More Time" the song hit number one for the first time. By March, Britney had the number-one song in more than twenty countries. That's a massive moment for any artist, but it was unprecedented for a woman making her debut—Spears was the first new female artist in history to have a song atop the *Billboard* 100 and an album atop the *Billboard* 200 at the same time. By the end of that year, she was the bestselling artist of 1999, with the biggest song and album in the world.

The schoolgirl look was a stroke of brilliant iconography. It was an instant Halloween costume, and it effectively became Spears's avatar in popular culture. But it also made Spears into a teenage sex symbol. And coming at a time when culture was loudly working through seemingly endless hang-ups around sex and women's bodies, her self-presentation was taken as an invitation to filter all those hang-ups through her. In April 1999, she was on the cover of *Rolling Stone,* lying on her back on a bed in pink satin underwear, holding a corded phone in one hand and clutching the purple Teletubby Tinky Winky in the other. That choice was an intentional one by the photographer David LaChapelle. At the time, Tinky Winky was embroiled in his own early-aughts morality play: The televangelist Jerry Falwell had attacked the character in a sermon for being "a gay role model." (What he meant by that is that Tinky Winky carries a purse.) LaChapelle was pushing the buttons of a reactionary strain in culture that was present around the turn of the century, and wound up as the backdrop to Spears's rise.

The headline on the cover story read: "Britney Spears, Teen

Queen. Inside the Heart and Mind (and Bedroom) of Britney," set in blockish letters against the pink satin of Spears's sheets. (Other headlines from the cover included "Bill Maher: What He Won't Say on TV" and "Norm Macdonald: Ready or Not For Prime Time?") *Shockingly,* it was the bedroom part that got all the attention—the first line of the article includes a reference to Spears's "honeyed thigh." I'm going to choose not to expose you to the several books' worth of examples of barf-worthy coverage of a teenaged Spears, from leering interviewers to gratuitously bitchy early-internet bloggers to condescending music industry veterans to *fucking Jay Leno,* but, as you can imagine, that reference was not an outlier.

A lot of that reaction came allegedly under the banner of concern about the example Spears was setting for other young people, which I have to say I find disingenuous. I wasn't tapped in on ". . . Baby One More Time" when it was released in real time, but a few years into Spears's career, I became obsessed. What I can say is that what I found interesting about her wasn't primarily about sex, or at least it wasn't any more about sex than anything else I thought was interesting! The fantasy she presented to girls was about independence, agency, and self-expression. Her performance, to me, was not a display of her body for its own sake but of the time-honored tradition of young women imagining themselves as adults. The extent to which this involved an interest in sexuality was unremarkable—like a girl stashing copies of *Cosmo* under her bed long before even having a first kiss and who'd been to plenty of sleepovers where girls started talking about their bodies as soon as parents closed a door and said good night. Teenage girls, generally speaking, are freaky weirdos! Britney wasn't introducing me to anything I wasn't already interested in; she just looked really cool doing it.

But as LaChapelle seemed to get, to older audiences, Spears's combination of innocence and provocation was what made her a sensation and set her apart from her teen pop predecessors. It wasn't just that Spears wore revealing clothes, or alluded to sex, it was the fact that she used the imagery of girlhood to do so that was fuel for a growing number of culture war debates. By the time she released her second major hit, "Oops! . . . I Did It Again," in 2000, the tagline of that song—*I'm not that innocent*—served to define Spears's persona. Spears's breakout happened to come just in the wake of Bill Clinton's impeachment trial in 1998, a watershed event for sex as a discussion topic even at dinner tables and in typically highbrow parts of media. It became common, for instance, for well-known journalists and outlets to ask young stars if they were virgins, a question Spears got many times. Tabloid journalism was becoming especially vulgar and emboldened and had a particular taste for young female stars like Spears who moved magazines much faster than boy band heartthrobs ever could. The members of *NSYNC and Backstreet were love objects, sure, but they weren't sexualized the way that Spears was as a teenager.

And Spears leaned in. Her knack for provocation set her apart from her nineties teen pop peers, but it had one obvious reference point in Madonna. And for the 2003 Video Music Awards, MTV asked Britney to be part of a performance with the Queen of Pop herself, a throwback to the inaugural VMAs in 1984, which Madonna had opened with a writhing rendition of "Like a Virgin" dressed in full bridal regalia, celebrating the show's history as a platform for provocation. As the curtain rose to the "Like a Virgin" intro, the symbolism was familiar. Two flower girls in white dresses—one of them Madonna's own daughter, Lourdes—walked down an aisle scattering rose petals in front of a massive layered wedding cake. On top of the cake stood a woman in a wedding dress and veil. Around her waist was a belt with the word "BOYTOY" on the buckle—another nod to the original, though only the original *Queer Eye* cast in the audience seemed to really get it. When the verse began, the woman lifted her veil, revealing that it was not Madonna on top of the cake but Britney Spears, fittingly presented as pop star heir apparent.

Britney sang the first verse as she descended the layers of the cake to the stage. When the chorus came around there was another surprise—a *second* bride in the same dress/veil/BOYTOY belt ensemble came out from behind the cake who turned out to be Christina Aguilera. The two sang the chorus and recreated the original stage-humping choreography (in the audience, Snoop Dogg gives a big thumbs-up) before turning back to the cake as the song faded away. Finally, the groom—Madonna, in a Dolce & Gabbana tux and top hat—emerges from the cake to perform her new single, "Hollywood."

Madonna doesn't actually perform any of "Like a Virgin." But she couldn't have paid tribute to her original performance without doing something to cause a stir. Three-quarters of the way through "Hollywood," Madonna bent down, removed a garter from around Aguilera's thigh, and tossed it into the audience. She then turned to Spears, stroked the side of her face, tilted her chin up, and planted a big, wet kiss on her lips. It was an open-mouthed passing of the baton: *I now pronounce you provocateur.* Of course, the crowd, the cameras, the papers, the pundits . . . they all went wild. The cameras panned immediately to Justin Timberlake, looking sour in the audience. The *New York Post* rushed to call the kiss "raunchy," "explicit," and—*gasp*—"open-mouth." *Us Weekly* ran a cover story speculating that they were actually an item. The whole thing caused enough of a fuss that Madonna herself wound up in a sit-down with Oprah. "I don't know if most of America has seen that before," Winfrey remarked, meaning two women kissing.

Spears took influence from the past, from Madonna in how she leveraged provocation and spectacle and, musically, from nineties teen pop, Robyn, and Max Martin. But when she mixed them together, melding both youthful and adult influences, she created the special sauce that kicked off a new cultural decade, captivating *TRL* teens and cultural critics alike. Almost instantly, or at least it felt that way, her aesthetic choices permeated youth culture, the racks at The Limited and Claire's suddenly stocked with clothes that looked like they were pulled from her videos. Likewise, in the music industry itself, her success placed a renewed focus on pop music at the start of the 2000s. There may not have been much pop on the charts just before Britney broke out but, once she did, that changed fast.

Nearly every tentpole figure of the aughts in and around pop music owes something to Britney, from working with Max Martin to create a hit, to learning to walk the line of provocateur/innocent. She is the figurehead of one of the more impressive freshman classes of pop stars in music history and her success paved the way for the dance-pop of Christina Aguilera, Mandy Moore, JoJo, Stacy Orrico, and other artists who would thrive at the start of the decade. Spears defined a new era of pop stardom and she inspired both copycats and, eventually, changes in the genre that came in response to her. It's fitting, really. She has always known how to get a reaction.

2

The Freshman
Class of Y2K

THE YEAR 1967 PROBABLY HAS THE BEST CASE FOR THE
strongest collection of debuts in the history of popular recorded
music, which began in earnest in the 1950s. That year brought us
Jimi Hendrix, Janis Joplin, Van Morrison, David Bowie, the Grateful Dead, Pink Floyd, the Velvet Underground, Sly and the Family
Stone, and Al Green. The collective rankings of those artists on
Rolling Stone's 100 Greatest Artists of All Time are higher than any
other year dating back to 1949 when Fats Domino, the earliest artist to appear on the list, put out his first album. The best years for
pop debuts came, of course, in the eighties, with Celine Dion and
Duran Duran joining Stevie Nicks, George Strait, Phil Collins, and
Mötley Crüe as significant entries in 1981 and Madonna herself
and Cyndi Lauper joining Metallica and R.E.M. in 1983. Those
years represented the last major wave of female pop solo acts hitting
the music scene, until 1999.

This was the Baby One More Time Boom, a group of female pop

artists who gained attention in Spears's wake and who, along with her, helped pop repopulate the charts and expand its sonic footprint. In the year following Spears's breakout hit, the music industry apparatus sprinted to find, sign, and market more young women in pop, hoping they'd capture the same rapt audience she had. Five months after Spears's January 1999 release of her debut album, Jennifer Lopez came out with hers, titled *On the 6*. Macy Gray's *On How Life Is,* led by the single "I Try," and Christina Aguilera's eponymous debut came later that summer. Jessica Simpson released hers, *Sweet Kisses,* in November and Mandy Moore closed out the year with *So Real* in December. These albums have stood the test of time to varying degrees, but each went platinum. Spears, Aguilera, and Gray made up three of the five nominees for Best New Artist at the Grammys in 2000, a category eventually won by Aguilera, representing a freshman class of Y2K pop stars that could rival any year. Although Spears's arrival had given the aughts a defining pop star, this group of peers popping up in her wake created an ecosystem that ensured pop music remained in focus on *TRL,* at awards shows, and on Top 40 radio for years to come. And while many of their careers were at first modeled after Spears's, these women's eventual efforts to distinguish themselves as individuals helped pop evolve musically beyond the Max Martin–produced dance-pop that began it all.

Perhaps this is ungenerous, but a quick perusal of record label decision-making from 1999 to 2000 seems to reveal a strategy that amounted to: (1) Find young woman, preferably blond. (2) Make her look, act, and sing as much like Britney Spears as possible. (3) Profit! The title track of Simpson's *Sweet Kisses,* a diluted R&B paean to love at any price that rhymes "riches" with "kisses," was offered to Spears, who recorded a demo version of the song before declining to include it on . . . *Baby One More Time*. Simpson's rich, church-crooner voice is a better fit for the song than Spears's, and yet, on the opening lines you hear her straining to tinge her "oh"s with a bit of Spearsian vocal fry. On the album cover itself, Simpson appears from the shoulders up. Instead of her normal big Texan blowout, her hair is pin straight and striped with chunky platinum highlights—exactly how Britney wore hers. She looks uncannily like her. And despite the fact that fifteen-year-old Mandy Moore showed up to her label audition talking about her love of Karen Carpenter and her desire to perform on Broadway, the Sony team that signed her suggested the dance-pop track "Candy," full of "oh, ohhhs, yeah yeah, yeah yeahs!" and a breathy, spoken-word bridge—as was quickly, by that point, becoming pop girl tradition—as her first single. Paired with its music video, which includes Mandy skateboarding in capris and getting milkshakes with her friends, it's the middle school equivalent of the high school, no-adults-to-be-found fantasy takeover of ". . . Baby One More Time." It is also—*and I cannot stress this enough*—a perfect song, though Moore did not feel so sure at the time it was perfect *for her.*

Lopez had the benefit of a successful movie career before she signed a record deal, so she arrived at pop stardom as more of a known quantity. Her big break had been 1997's *Selena,* where she became the first Latina actress to earn over $1 million for a film. Still, she wasn't immune to the post-Britney dynamics of the industry. In 1999, with Lopez interested in multihyphenate stardom and in getting back onstage, her manager Benny Medina circulated a Spanish-language demo in search of a record deal. When the demo reached Tommy Mottola, though, he suggested she perform in English, with a dance-pop sound. That led to *On the 6,* with the Hot 100–topping single "If You Had My Love" and the top-ten "Waiting for Tonight." *On the 6* also contains the barn-burning "Let's Get Loud," a phrase which Lopez worked into the medley of "This

Land Is Your Land" and "America the Beautiful" she performed at Joe Biden's presidential inauguration in 2021, because a Leo will never let a microphone go to waste.

"Waiting For Tonight" was nominated for Best Dance Recording at the 2000 Grammys, an event to which Lopez showed up in her iconic green plunging Versace gown, a look that led to the creation of Google Images. Lopez went on to release eight studio albums of Latin-inflected dance-pop, sell more than eighty million records, headline two world tours, co-headline two massive tours geared toward a Latine audience with Marc Anthony and Enrique Iglesias, and put on a Las Vegas residency that ran for two years and made over $100 million, easily making her one of the most successful pop artists of the decade. Lopez didn't struggle to define herself relative to Spears, because of her appeal to Spanish-speaking audiences and because being a pop star wasn't how she became famous, but Spears's popularity likely influenced the sound of *On the 6*, still some of Lopez's most loved work.

While JLo didn't have to work too hard to avoid the Britney comparisons, Christina Aguilera was a different story. Really, she never had a chance. They just have too much in common. She and Britney were both childhood talent show contestants who'd made their way onto *Star Search* only to lose, which turns out to be a pretty good way to become super, super famous (among Ed McMahon's other whiffs, in addition to Britney and Xtina, was Girl's Tyme, the precursor to Destiny's Child). They were *Mickey Mouse Club* castmates (which also turned out to be a good way to become super, super famous). And yeah, okay, they were blond and showed some midriff. What's it to you?

What those comparisons meant to RCA Records when ". . . Baby One More Time" came out in 1998 just as Aguilera was noodling on an R&B album was a change in direction. Once the label saw

Britney's success working with Max Martin and doing dance-pop, they nudged Aguilera to do the same. Aguilera wanted her first single to be a soaring ballad in the tradition of her idol Mariah Carey's "Vision of Love." But Ron Fair, the RCA A&R man who'd championed Aguilera at the label and won her a significant amount of resources and attention in support of her debut, convinced her to start with dance-pop because he was sure that's what would break her out. When he heard a demo for a song called "If You Wanna Be with Me," an up-tempo track about love and self-respect and also maybe—wink, wink—about sex, he fought hard for that, too, securing the track for Aguilera over Paula Abdul and the girl group Innosense. He also suggested that a different lyric would make for a better title: "Genie in a Bottle."

The record was a massive success. *Christina Aguilera* had a whopping three number-one hits in 1999: "Genie in a Bottle," the addictive dance hit with its Spears-indebted vocal treatment (and its Spears-indebted teenager-sings-come-hither-song vibe), the peppy "What a Girl Wants," and my personal favorite, the wickedly fun "Come On Over (All I Want Is You)." The album debuted at number one and was certified eight times platinum in the US, ultimately selling over seventeen million copies worldwide. It made Aguilera a massive star, a fixture on *TRL* just like Britney. What it didn't make her was happy with the direction her music career was going. If you listened closely, you could hear this even within the biggest and most successful tracks off *Christina Aguilera*. "What a Girl Wants" is a bop that both cleared the one-hit-wonder bar for Aguilera and secured the top Y2K honor of soundtracking an Amanda Bynes rom-com by the same name, in which Bynes travels to England in search of the father she has never known, who turns out to be Colin Firth playing a British Earl of Somethingorother. Hijinks ensue! I remember *What a Girl Wants* as a perfect movie, though, as I write this, I'm scanning the *Rotten Tomatoes* page, and in order to keep it that way I think I'll skip the rewatch. Anyway, listen closely to "What a Girl Wants" and you can hear the dueling points of view. You can hear the Martin-esque efficiency of the track, the shiny synthesizer pulses, and the syncopated drum machines fighting with the metric tons of melisma and vocal acrobatics Aguilera wants to smash into a three-minute song. Ever see a racehorse in the starting gate before a race, frantic to run? That's Christina on "What a Girl Wants." The energy is impressive, and it's not like there's no point to the gate structure, either. But she's not really supposed to be in there. There had been an earlier version of "What a Girl Wants" on the album before it was rereleased as a single (which ultimately went to number one), recorded at a slower tempo with more space in the production and more of a true R&B sound, but Fair once again wanted it to sound more like a Max Martin tune—hookier, stickier, and brighter.

After "What a Girl Wants," RCA let Aguilera release her ballad—a cover of the Diane Warren–penned "I Turn to You," which made it to number three. But Fair felt like there was one more song from her debut they could remix and rerelease and squeeze some dance-pop juice out of, and he turned out to be right. "Come On Over" was a song on *Christina Aguilera* that had been written for her by a team of Swedish songwriters named Paul Rein and Johan Åberg who were part of a songwriting collective in Stockholm that was attempting to recreate what Max Martin had at Cheiron. On the original album, Aguilera just rerecorded the vocal to the instrumentals from the demo track, but to update the production and the lyrics, Fair brought in a stable of writers. The finished track has a CVS receipt's worth of credits on it, and there's no great reason why. Both versions sound fine. They're both pretty pop friendly. To be honest, the main difference is that they added the line where

Aguilera talks about her *sexualitayyyyy,* and maybe that was worth doing. Fair reportedly wanted the song to be sexier. Christina didn't have a lot of bubblegum left in her. She was decreasingly content to go in the direction that Fair and RCA wanted her to and increasingly adamant about singing R&B, enough that the constant remixing of her early songs comes across as an attempt to placate multiple factions. Perhaps the final straw was the 2003 VMAs performance with Spears and Madonna, in which Aguilera's own kiss with Madonna was cut out of the broadcast in favor of a reaction shot from Justin Timberlake. In the aftermath of that show, former MTV executive vice president Tom Calderone told *Rolling Stone* that Aguilera's team asked the network to reedit Christina's kiss back in on future broadcasts, though they did not. Aguilera had already begun a musical pivot by that point, but it's easy to see how that experience would have reinforced the need for her to define herself outside of Spears's shadow. As Aguilera was rethinking her musical direction, pop music itself was morphing. Though the post-Britney influx of talented stars and great songs prolonged the era of teen pop, the boy bands and girl groups had already waned and the stars who wanted to stay relevant needed to evolve. Even Spears herself was approaching a transition point—her third album, 2001's *Britney,* failed to get a single inside the top ten and sales were relatively soft. Rap was bigger than ever, even among mainstream, mostly white audiences. At the 2001 Grammys, Eminem won Best Rap Solo Performance for "The Real Slim Shady," a song that manages to put Britney Spears, Christina Aguilera, boy bands, *and* girl groups in his crosshairs. Mr. Shady's top target was Aguilera, based on some personal beef stemming from her 1999 MTV special *What a Girl Wants,* in which she'd gossiped that Em and his longtime girlfriend, Kim, might be married (and shaded the fact that he rapped a murder fantasy about Christina which, to be fair, was always a little much!), but his lyrical diatribe ended on a related, but different note:

> *I'm sick of you little girl and boy groups*
> *All you do is annoy me, so I have been sent here to destroy you*

On this crusade I would argue that Em was only partially successful. It's not his fault. If we take him literally, then, yes, boy bands and girl groups did go out of vogue right around the time that hip-hop surged. If that statement was meant to lump in the Spearses and Aguileras of the world, though, Slim Shady came up short. The extremes did arrive, dominated by Eminem and his contemporaries and bubblegum's pop-punk counterweights like Avril Lavigne, but pop—and Spears and Aguilera themselves—continued to evolve.

Before she released her sophomore pop album, 2002's *Stripped*, Aguilera took a full three years off to redirect. "The music I was making on my first album, I was still very much under the thumb of a lot of older men and women," she told *Rolling Stone*. Between her first and second records, Aguilera fired her manager, hired industry veteran Irving Azoff, and released a Spanish-language record as well as the hit of the *Moulin Rouge!* soundtrack, "Lady Marmalade," with Pink, Lil' Kim, and Mýa. It was in some ways a risky choice not to immediately capitalize on the success of *Christina Aguilera*—Spears had released three albums by the time *Stripped* came out—but Aguilera was determined to change directions. However delicious, one thing her debut album did not do was take full advantage of Aguilera's voice, with its four-octave range, grit, and natural soul. "Lady Marmalade" previewed what an asset this could be, and *Stripped* leaned further in. "Fighter" levels up from simple catchiness on the strength of the texture Aguilera brings to the vocal, and the ballad "Beautiful" became a career-defining hit that reflected Aguilera's sheer ability and insistence on sticking up for what she believed was right. The album was not exclusively well-received—the song "Dirrty," featuring the rapper Redman, and particularly its David LaChapelle–directed music video depicting sexual fetishes from mud wrestling to muscle worship surprised even Aguilera with how much controversy it generated. "It made me sad how conservative and judgmental a lot of people were, and I was never coming on the scene to impose anything upon anyone. I just wanted to live my life and not conform," Aguilera said. But that nonconformist streak was one she wound up embracing as Aguilera zigged into her next era with the soul-, blues-, and jazz-inflected record *Back to Basics,* then zagged toward futuristic electro-pop with *Bionic.*

Others found their own lanes, too. Lopez embraced Latin dance music more wholeheartedly. Simpson had more success leaning into gospel and by starting to promote her music via her role in the budding reality TV industry. It began with a special featuring Simpson and her then husband Nick Lachey, *Newlyweds: Nick & Jessica,* that helped boost her third album *In This Skin.* Moore mostly turned away from music and toward TV and movies, though she did use her voice in her iconic turn in *The Princess Diaries.* There were others who never really found their own footing—the singer Willa Ford enjoyed a post-Britney fifteen minutes on the strength of her first single "I Wanna Be Bad," which lives on as a Y2K playlist staple, but her career stalled when her second single flopped, in large part due to its release on 9/11.

In the end, though, it was still Britney herself who proved the most versatile. By the time the 2003 VMAs rolled around, long after Eminem declared boy bands and girl groups to be DOA, Spears was entering her fourth album cycle and adjusting her sound. Her second album, the triumphant *Oops!. . . I Did It Again,* mostly followed up on . . . *Baby One More Time*'s successful formulas, from Max Martin down to the ellipsis. But from *Britney* on, she began trying on new sounds, particularly from the world of hiphop, which was exploding—the top songs of the previous year had included Ashanti's "Foolish"; Nelly's "Hot in Herre" and "Dilemma," featuring Kelly Rowland; Usher's "U Got It Bad"; and Mary J. Blige's "Public Affair." The lead single for *Britney,* "I'm a Slave 4 U," was not produced by Martin but by Chad Hugo and Pharrell Williams, known as the production duo the Neptunes. There were still several Martin tracks on *Britney,* including one of their very best collaborations in "Overprotected," which teemed with enough bass and snare for an entire album. But the album showcased a Spears that wasn't dependent on the teen pop Cheironproduced sound she'd broken out with, and the lead single hinted at where she'd go next. If *Britney* seeded the idea that Spears could change with the times, her fourth album, *In the Zone,* and the smash hit "Toxic" completed her realignment.

"Toxic" doesn't exactly sound like early-2000s pop hip-hop—it doesn't really sound like *anything* recognizable from the pop charts at the time. It begins with high, whining strings sampled from the soundtrack of a Bollywood movie called *Ek Duuje Ke Liye* chopped and spliced into an ominous refrain that repeats throughout the song. Then the verse comes in, the lyrics telling a story of giving in to temptation set against musical text painting of that internal conflict. The whole song fights itself: Crunchy acoustic guitars battle the fuzzy, electronic baseline. Dark, chromatic chords tangle with a bright and shiny melody. The song is wrought with tension. After each pre-chorus come eight full beats of staticky guitar power chords, an eternity in a pop song—certainly not something Max Martin would have approved. But to hear "Toxic" is to be on the edge of your seat before the chorus arrives, delivering Britney's vocals engaged in a call-and-response with a surf guitar adding to the James Bondian thrill of it all. The song was Spears's favorite. "The way [it was produced] musically was very cool, and really different, that's why I liked it so much," Spears told MTV.

According to the producer Bloodshy, Zomba thought it was too weird to be a single, maybe even too weird to go on the record had Spears not put her foot down. Perhaps not since she tied up her shirt while filming ". . . Baby One More Time" had Spears's intuition that something would work been so spot on. *In the Zone* had the lucky timing of being released six months after Apple launched the iTunes Music Store, and digital downloads became a quick indicator that "Toxic" was a standout despite being relatively hidden at track six on the album. Zomba quickly agreed to make it the second single, and "Toxic" became Spears's fourth top-ten hit, her best-performing song since "Oops! . . . I Did It Again." Perhaps more importantly, the song became a critical and indie darling, one that got Spears a kind of legitimate respect as a musician that had thus far dodged her. To date, her only Grammy award is for "Toxic," which won Best Dance Recording of 2004. And yet again, Britney had provided a harbinger of one of the next musical moments, presaging an electro-pop wave that was about to hit. NPR, which named *In the Zone* among its fifty most important recordings of the decade, called it "a primer on the sound of pop in the '00s," and "the ideal vehicle for a futuristic sound." At a time when Eminem himself had predicted her downfall, when pop punk was supposedly coming to end the vapid princesses who didn't write their own songs, Britney didn't vanish but instead simply changed music yet again.

It had to be frustrating, right? To be one of the many pop stars who followed in Spears's footsteps and wound up stuck in her shadow? And yet, Spears's success was undeniably responsible for the surge in resources and enthusiasm for young, female pop singers around the year 2000. And it was the way Spears's contemporaries bumped up against her and fought to find their own paths, ultimately, that began to broaden the scope of possible versions of pop stardom out from Spears's original blueprint. Not only was Spears responsible for creating the model for a pop star in the aughts, but she also challenged her contemporaries to continue to evolve as she herself experimented with genre and adapted to new trends. What resulted was a pop wave that lasted far beyond the teen pop cycle defined by Britney, then Christina and everyone else just before the turn of the century, one that was richer, more varied, and less easily dismissed as a fad.

3

Avril Esta Morta

IT'S 2004, AND CARSON DALY IS STIRRING THE POT BE-
cause he is messy and he lives for drama. He's standing in front of
what I believe is the purple-, citron-yellow-, and aquamarine-
painted *Real World* house in Key West, Florida, and however wide
you think his pant legs are, I promise you, they are wider than that.
Strangely enough, I have slept in that exact house, as it's now available as a Vrbo rental targeting bachelorette parties and, I must
imagine, cocaine benders. I attended for the former, and can therefore attest that it has a zebra-print hot tub in the living room and
several framed newspaper articles on the walls about how the original owner committed extortion, and that if you have approximately
four watermelon margaritas, jump in the pool, and demand to hear
"Despacito" on repeat you can have a really great time there. Anyway, Carson is standing on the deck of the house holding a microphone and an index card, which you know means trouble. Behind

him is an assemblage of a few dozen women sitting scattered across the house's porch, most of them in bathing suits or tube tops and daisy dukes. Next to him, in a muscle tank and jeans, pin-straight hair and thick black eyeliner holding up admirably in the humidity, is a nineteen-year-old Avril Lavigne, about to be lightly bludgeoned with her own words.

"Hey, um, okay, so there's this whole thing going on on the internet that you hate Britney Spears," Daly begins. This is how he *begins* the interview. "Let me read this quote and if you want you can comment on it or do whatever you want with it, but here's what we found." (Thank you, Carson, how very generous.)

Avril furrows her brow and scrunches up her nose but is helpless to escape. Nothing but manatees and self-tanner for miles around. Daly turns to his index cards.

"This is you talking about Britney," he says again.

> *"Would you walk around the street in an effing bra? She's not being herself up there because she's dancing like a ho. Is she a ho? She says she's a virgin. You know, it's just not clicking."*

"End quote, Avril Lavigne on Britney Spears," Daly says. "What's the deal?"

By this point, the audience is in a frenzy. This is '04 MTV. Talking about who is or is not a "ho" is core programming. The audience started to clap right around the first "ho," and had been whipped into a full froth by "virgin." That they are in Key West, not merely walking around the streets in garments not dissimilar to bras and underwear but also appearing on television that way is apparently lost on everyone involved.

Avril, in her nasal Ontario drawl, mounts her defense:

"I feel like the press kind of likes to stick words in artists' mouths and kind of, like, exaggerate on things," she says, a fair claim were it not for the fact that she had indeed given the exact quote on BBC Radio. "I said I'm different from her."

Daly prods: "Did you say she dances like a ho?" His button-down shirt is untucked and so oversized it hits at his knees.

"No!" Avril squeals, before devolving into awkward, guilty laughter.

"Just a little bit, you said that," Daly says gleefully.

Avril then gets serious: "Yo! I'm not dissing her, and I don't mean to diss any artist because, I mean, I don't need to do that. She's doing her thing and I'm doing mine and that's all I have to say."

It was not, as it turned out, all she had to say. Avril, around this time, had a habit of distinguishing herself from her musical contemporaries by putting them down. Ahead of a BBC Radio 1 performance in 2004, Lavigne told *The Sunday Mail* that "Britney and Christina Aguilera were groomed for stardom and turned into sex symbols. I wasn't," and that "There are so many artists who just get some songwriter to do all the work that people are skeptical about what they hear these days," but that she wrote her own stuff. She didn't have a lot of great things to say about women in general. In high school, Lavigne said, "Most girls were trying to become the next beauty queen but I was more interested in doing skateboard stunts and kicking ass."

There is no arguing the final point. Avril Lavigne kicks a *considerable* amount of ass. I'm also willing to buy she knows her way around a skate park. The first few, though, require some qualification. We can leave sex symbols out of it for now, but let's be extremely clear that Avril Lavigne was groomed for stardom. At the age of sixteen, Lavigne, having gained attention when she won a radio contest that chose a young singer to perform a duet with Shania Twain, was signed to a $1.2 million, two-album deal with Arista Records, plus a $900,000 publishing advance, on the strength of a fifteen-minute audition for label head L.A. Reid. Britney and Christina might have had a few years of Mousketeering on her, but Avril Lavigne was quite clearly a product of the major-label system.

Why, then, was Lavigne so intent on proving she had nothing in common with them? The answer has to do with genre, double standards, and the music industrial value system coming out of its 1990s obsession with alternative rock, a love affair that cast a long shadow on pop in the 2000s and over artists like Lavigne who used rock aesthetics in particular. It has to do with one of the lasting impacts of Lavigne's career, which was to shed light on the ways in which pop was still looked down upon and the ways in which female artists were pressured to stay in narrow lanes. It has to do with a relitigation of what it meant to be an "authentic" artist at a moment when commercial interests were reasserting themselves even in punkish spaces that traditionally spurned them. It might have had to do with the fact that Avril Lavigne didn't like Britney Spears that much. But if you want to boil all that down into one simple reason, it's this: Avril Lavigne didn't want to be branded a big, phony sellout.

As an artist who mixed pop, punk rock, and singer-songwriter influences, Lavigne's career serves as a reminder of how "authenticity" in music was used as a cudgel, especially against pop stars, and ultimately as a lesson in how arbitrarily those criticisms were applied. After her 2002 debut album, *Let Go,* was a smash success based on its rock-inflected hooks and earnest mall punk lyrics, Lavigne found herself in a delicate position as the new female face of pop punk in a moment when many argued that was a contradiction in terms. That moment came as the music world was getting ready for a conversation about whether it was productive to evaluate pop stars gunning for chart placements and *TRL* spots by rock standards of rebellion and disaffection. Lavigne did not start that conversation herself; that was ultimately done by one of her musical offspring. But as she discovered quickly, pure pop stars like Britney and Christina might have had to prove themselves as more than bubblegum juvenilia, but no one faced more musical purity tests in the early aughts than a pop star who looked like a rock star.

When *Let Go* arrived in 2002, the Swedish hit parade led by Britney, Christina, and the boy bands was dying down. It had been three years since Spears's debut, and Britney herself was already transitioning away from teen pop. For her third album, *Britney Spears,* she chose "I'm a Slave 4 U," an R&B-inflected dance number produced by hip-hop power duo the Neptunes as the lead single over the Max Martin–produced "Overprotected," which shared the orchestral hits and tight structure of their earlier hits. Aguilera was also getting ready for her own shift away from teen pop. Radio stations were yearning for hits and for some new texture. Zapoleon, the Top 40 whisperer, says that pop stations are happiest when pure pop makes up about 35 percent of the *Billboard* Top 100. From 2001 to 2004, though, the genre dwindled down to representing only 17 percent of the songs people really liked. There was a wideopen lane for something pop, it just had to be something different from what Britney and all the boy bands—with their programmed drums, choreographed dance moves, and Scandi producers—had been doing up to that point, and in came Lavigne.

If an artist like Aguilera struggled to *differentiate* herself from Spears, Lavigne, in her baggy pants and heavy eyeliner, singing heartfelt songs about being a teenage outcast, was immediately cast in contrast to Britney and teen pop. The press started calling her the "anti-Britney," a nickname that, best I can tell, appeared for the first time in an *Entertainment Weekly* profile from November of 2002 that began this way:

> Ciao, Britney! Skanks—er, thanks—for the memories, Christina. How were you to know that, come the end of 2002, the girls of America would no longer be lowering their necklines in homage to you but, instead, learning how to knot a necktie?

The piece keeps going from there! There's a lot to unpack. There's a line about butt cheeks and dance beats being out and tank tops and "real" being in. There's some pretty pervasive casual sexism, and a lot of sweeping judgments made in passive voice. "Pop tarts" are allegedly toast, though according to who, exactly, is not clear. Even that nickname, "the anti-Britney," is credited to Lavigne's fans generally, though to me it sounds a lot more like a media or industry idea.

These were the days of *Mean Girls* and Perez Hilton, and cultural discourse in general celebrated bitchiness to the point that tonally, those passages were par for the course in a major magazine—and for as much cringe as they inspire now, there's also something juicy and fun about the unabashed Burn Book quality that comes through. Cattiness aside, it's revealing to read those paragraphs for what they say about how Lavigne was positioned and perceived relative to her peers. She's described as a "female singer-songwriter," despite the fact that Lavigne did not write songs on her own. She's credited with bringing "rock" back, despite the fact that Lavigne's songs were mostly targeted to pop radio. She's compared to alt-rockers like Courtney Love and the Pretenders' Chrissie Hynde. The urge to compare Lavigne and Spears in the first place gives up some understanding of them as peers, but perhaps because it wouldn't hold up without the contrast, the image of Lavigne painted in the relief of her contemporaries was as the new female face of punk rock.

To her credit, in her interview for that *EW* piece, Lavigne rejected the binary. "I don't like that term—'the anti-Britney.' It's stupid," she said. "I don't believe in that. She's a human being. God, leave her alone."

It might have saved her a lot of trouble if Lavigne could have responded to every question about Spears that way. She did not. At the time, Lavigne had a very severe case of "not like other girls" syndrome that tended to manifest itself in some *wild* quotes. She once said that if she ever did a movie it couldn't be "a Mandy Moore kind of movie, a chick flick. I have to do, like, a *Girl, Interrupted.*" (I think I can say confidently we're all better off for this never having happened.) The entire plot of "Sk8er Boi" is basically designed to dunk on a girl because she didn't want to go out with some dude in high school. And she loved to talk about Britney Spears, about her clothes, about her dancing, about her relationships. She joined the chorus of voices speculating about Spears's virginity, a topic of national interest particularly during and after Spears's relationship with Justin Timberlake. (Britney never really engaged with Avril, other than one *W* magazine interview in 2003 when she said: "Avril doesn't really dance, but whatever. It's weird. My third album sold as much as her first one which is very funny to me because everyone thought it didn't do that great." It is *so* Britney that she made it about dancing.)

It's possible Lavigne was merely speaking out of a deeply felt distaste for choreography and hot pants. More likely, I imagine she was to some extent just responding to her environment, where girl-on-girl crime and slut-shaming were richly rewarded in attention.

Lavigne had also professed her virginity, because that's something we regularly used to make singers do! But the other reason she went after Spears was that the Lavigne sales pitch had been decided: She was a punk, they did ballet. "I created punk for this day and age," she told *Seventeen* in 2002. "Do you see Britney walking around wearing ties and singing punk? Hell no. That's what I do. I'm like a Sid Vicious for a new generation."

Every part of that is hysterical and awesome. A seventeen-year-old Avril Lavigne saying in the pages of—checks notes—*Seventeen* magazine that she created punk. The phrase "walking around and singing punk." *A Sid Vicious for a new generation.* We need more pop stars comparing themselves to the Sex Pistols. That is the good stuff. I loved Sid Vicious's spreads in *Tiger Beat.*

She wasn't completely off base in drawing a distinction between herself and Spears. Lavigne's point of view as an angsty teenager was intrinsic to the music she recorded in a way that those of Spears or Aguilera weren't in their early music. Britney embodied her songs through personality, but usually not through autobiography—the song "Toxic," for instance, is written in the second person, but I never hear it and wonder who it's about, since what "Toxic" is about is being young and hot and kind of horny. Lavigne, on the other hand, generally sang songs that sounded like they were about experiences she had, or at least *could* have had. She was also involved in her own songwriting process, which Spears really wasn't for her first two albums. So there were genuine differences. Still, they were not nearly as pronounced as the coverage implies. Lavigne and Spears both grew up singing in church, they were both swept out of small-town life for stardom very young due to their immense talents. Both of them recorded music engineered for success on Top 40 radio; neither of them was the type of songwriter to sit down at the piano and come away with a whole new composition. Lavigne might have been compared to artists like Vanessa Carlton and Michelle Branch, who were their own primary songwriters, but her actual process was somewhere in the middle, if not closer to the Spearsian end of things.

One could actually make an argument that Lavigne had a fair point when she called her music "punk for this day and age," because punk was having a weird go of things in the early aughts. Punk might not have been pop in the pure sense, but it was certainly popular, which meant that a genre that had defined itself by its antagonism toward the mainstream was now a major part of it. Bands that had come up through venerated punk scenes in places like Berkeley, California, had decided it was time to make some money and signed major-label deals; one of those bands, Green Day, was mainstream enough by the early 2000s that my middle school choir was covering "Good Riddance (Time of Your Life)" every year at the graduation ceremony. Others, like Blink-182, were punks who knew how to work pop systems to their benefit—in 2000, their "All the Small Things" music video spoofed those of the Backstreet Boys' "I Want It That Way," Britney Spears's "Sometimes," and Christina Aguilera's "Genie in a Bottle," but the entire *point* of that was that it would crush on *TRL,* which it did. Then there were bands like Good Charlotte, who'd had major-label deals all along, but were increasingly hard to distinguish from any of the other sorts of Hot Topic punks. That last description says it all. The genre of CBGB and Gilman Street was now associated with *the mall.*

I have to tell you that, when I was listening to Avril Lavigne for the first time, most if not all of this would have been news to me. If you'd lived through the nineties and were versed in that punk scene, you'd been taught that "selling out" was this huge deal for which bands were shunned—the Gilman Street venue, for instance, only allowed bands on indie labels, which led to a huge amount of drama when a group like Green Day signed a major-label contract. I'm sure if that was the case, mainstream pop punk was probably a major mindfuck. If you were too young to even know those cultural shibboleths, though, it really didn't matter. For better or worse, a lot of artists seemed to discover new patience for commercial interests about the time when Napster disrupted the music industry's financial model in 1999, and those of us who came of age after that point were probably less inclined to see that as damning. I don't remember ever thinking about who was or was not a "sellout" when I was first listening to Avril and the Warped Tour bands, and I don't think I'd have cared much even if I had. This is not to say that the downfall of the idea of selling out was necessarily a good thing; pop fans in general are probably too comfortable these days egging on artists, most commercial instincts. But the truth as I felt it was that no one really cared. Britney Spears was selling me Pepsi. I definitely didn't know who Sid Vicious was! Avril Lavigne wrote the songs I listened to when I wanted to stare out of the school bus window on my ride home feeling angsty, and that was punk enough for me.

Lavigne, however, wanted to rock like a true punk. So with the ink barely dry on her major-label deal, she began searching for the sound of her first album, which she wanted to take in a relatively hardcore direction. Her first partner was Cliff Magness, a Texas-born singer-songwriter and producer with whom she cowrote five tracks that wound up on *Let Go*: "Losing Grip," "Unwanted," "My World," "Too Much to Ask," and "Mobile." "Losing Grip" and "Unwanted," in particular, are two of the hardest-rocking guitar songs on the album and were among Lavigne's favorites. (She was in a big System of a Down phase, go figure.) Arista, however, was extremely *not* down for their burgeoning pop prodigy to veer so far into nu metal and sought out a different influence.

Word of Lavigne's situation had made its way to Sandy Roberton, a manager who represented a production trio called the Matrix, who were having moderate success producing mostly pop-R&B tracks for projects like Christina Aguilera's Christmas album or the first record by the Disney Records artist Myra, who you may know as the singer of *The Princess Diaries* title track "Miracles Happen." (Hector Elizondo you will *always* be famous!) Roberton suggested that the Matrix, whose three members were Scott Spock, Lauren Christy, and Graham Edwards, try writing with Avril. He may have had an inkling from the Arista side that the direction needed to work as pop, but he gave the same Faith Hill and Shania Twain touchpoints to Spock, Christy, and Edwards when he pitched them on working with her. That wasn't really their lane, but they were looking for work and decided to give it a go. When Lavigne showed up to their first session in a black T-shirt, punky braids, and a bracelet made of melted toothbrushes around her wrist, it became clear fast that that wasn't her lane, either.

Within a day or so of meeting, Lavigne and the Matrix cut the demo for the song "Complicated," still the best-known track of her career and the ultimate teen-angst manifesto, the perfect soundtrack to particularly high school problems that inspire great feeling over insignificant events. The demo was an instant hit at Arista headquarters; when L.A. Reid got it, he heard not just a single, but an identity. "Complicated" positioned Lavigne as a pop star with a punk aesthetic, sincere enough to read as a rebuttal to someone like Spears, but plenty capable of churning out sing-along hits that would work in the same radio and MTV formats that Spears's did. Reid called the members of the Matrix right after he heard the demo. "Whatever you've got there, that's it," he said. "She ain't no Shania Twain."

Reid suggested Lavigne move to Los Angeles temporarily to keep working with the Matrix. So she got on a plane and spent the summer in California fleshing out an album, often working out of the cramped one-bedroom in Studio City that Spock was renting at the time. The walls were covered in warped wood paneling, which made for a great recording space because their uneven surfaces eliminated bounces of sound that can create pings of feedback. They had a Neumann U87 microphone and a session guitar player named Corky James who Spock called his "human synthesizer" because of the large collection of amplifiers he'd drag over and experiment with, finding different sounds that threaded the pop needle and the punk one—but in that order of importance. "It's got to go on pop radio," Spock would say. "It can't be on the rock stations, we've got to pop it up." The solution was often big 808 drums, thick and booming enough that one of Spock's rap clients poked his head into a recording session for "Sk8er Boi," curious what he was hearing. Spock's goal for the song was that, when it gets "to the chorus, if you're listening in a car or on a big stereo, you're like, *where'd that bass come from?!* What's going on, this is a punk record!"

With "Complicated" and "Sk8er Boi" under their belt, the Matrix wanted to try for a ballad with Lavigne. They wound up recording "I'm with You," a big, emotive tribute to loneliness. The vocal is no joke—you may recognize the "yeah-ee-yeah, yeah-ee-yeahs" sampled in Rihanna's "Cheers (Drink to That)"—and Lavigne nails it. The actual vocal on the song comes from what was supposed to be a practice session at Spock's home studio but turned into the real thing when Lavigne's take gave everyone goosebumps. With "I'm with You" done, they had the first three singles for the album.

Two more songs Lavigne wrote with the Matrix made the cut for *Let Go* as well—the excellent "Anything but Ordinary," which Reid wanted to make the title track before Lavigne put her foot down, and "Things I'll Never Say," a relatively breezy story of unprofessed feelings. Lavigne fought for the harder-rocking songs she'd written with Magness to make the cut as well and got her way, but the songs with the Matrix were undeniable. Each of the three singles became top-ten hits and were largely responsible for the phenomenal success of the album, which has been certified platinum seven times over in just the United States. "Complicated" would have gone to number one under almost any circumstance, but it was blocked from the top spot by Nelly's "Hot in Herre," which was an immovable object atop the Hot 100 in the summer of 2002. Lavigne was the *next big thing*.

It was not just the songs that were popular, it was the look. Studded belts and Manic Panic hair dye were in. The Limited Too was stocking chokers. If the Spearsian brand of hyperfemininity felt particularly unattainable or unappealing, Lavigne's style was a welcome alternative. After reading my thirty-second magazine feature on how to "borrow from the boys," I raided my dad's closet for neckties. Once around this time, during a holiday shopping trip at the mall with my grandmother, I told her I needed to go to the bathroom and then snuck into a Hot Topic just to look around, but I got freaked out by the sex stuff and left immediately.

It might have been fine with me that Lavigne was a pop star in punk clothing, but the bigger she got the more her punk credentials started getting called into question. As *Let Go* racked up millions in sales and Lavigne earned Grammy nominations, including Best New Artist and Song of the Year, a *Rolling Stone* piece revealed conflicting stories over the authorship of "Complicated," with Lavigne saying she wrote the song herself, about the "tons of people in the world who are fake, who are two-faced," in the few hours after meeting the Matrix. "Songwriting is like that for me," she said. "Someone can say, 'Go write a song,' and I can do it. I can write a song in a day." The producers themselves, though, claimed they wrote the bulk of the song and then brought it to Lavigne, who made some minor lyrical tweaks, like changing *Take off all your stupid clothes* to *preppy clothes*. Spock remembers it as a collaboration, but one where the Matrix essentially brought Lavigne a draft and she gave edits. "She was singing along to it going, 'Yeah! This sounds good,' and she got involved in changing lyrics and figuring out the right melodies for her and stuff, and she was so into it," he said.

It's maybe a distinction without tons of difference. Spock said he loved working with Lavigne and that she was already an immensely talented artist who made significant contributions. ("Preppy clothes," for the record, is miles better than "stupid clothes.") As a matter of fact, the three members of the Matrix and Lavigne split songwriting royalties evenly and are all credited. But given that Lavigne's singer-songwriter credentials had been held up as a key part of her artistry, questions surrounding her authorship were damning. Her albums came with liner notes made to look handwritten, and though she didn't play an instrument herself, she sang with a band, making her vulnerable to a series of musical purity tests. At a Grammy nominations event that year, she mispronounced Davie Bowie's name (like Howie, instead of like doughy) and it became a whole thing. No one cared that Spears's songs of youthful expression were written by a bunch of anonymous Swedes, but Lavigne was selling authenticity (and comparing herself to Sid Vicious) when a lot of pop stars were selling fantasy. Lavigne didn't work with the Matrix again—Spock says no hard feelings—and when it came time for her second album, cowriting was a sensitive topic.

Perhaps in part because she'd been accused of aping its concept, Lavigne had come to feel that "Complicated" was a poor representation of her artistry. For her sophomore album, she badly wanted to lean into a harder sound. She had become close with her guitar player, a shaggy blond named Evan Taubenfeld who kept his day job working at the Apple Store Genius Bar while they worked on *Under My Skin*. They were both in their late teens and had left school early to pursue music careers, and Avril was thirsting for both a friend her own age and a pop-cultural education, both of which Evan could offer.

Evan was also friendly with Butch Walker, a glam-metal rocker from Georgia who'd just hit pop-punk payday with Bowling for Soup, producing the band's second major-label album, *Drunk Enough to Dance,* and the hit single "Girl All the Bad Guys Want." Evan suggested to Lavigne she might want to work with Walker. Walker was familiar with the situation with the Matrix and was a little wary of the dynamic—"I just thought it was kind of ugly," he told me in an interview—and wondered why it hadn't been kept behind-the-scenes.

"I was like, oh man, I understand that the label and management and everybody else is needing to establish credibility with this kid, so their whole angle was 'She wrote it all, she plays, she did it all,'" Walker said. "And whether that's true or not, it doesn't matter. It just felt really, to me, a little bit bitter having three older people coming after this girl that had a legion of ten million little girls for fans. Who do you think they're going to side with? They're not going to side with the three old writers! They're going to side with her."

Because of the heat from the Matrix stories, Arista initially told Walker not to even think about writing any lyrics for the record, that he wouldn't get credit and that he could only produce. Gradually, though, it became clear that some of Avril's compositions weren't working as completed songs, some of them missing bridges and entire sections. One evening, Walker decided to take a pen to one of them, an indignant ballad directed at some guy who thinks

Avril is going to hook up with him called "Don't Tell Me." And lo and behold, the song worked. Out of dozens that came from various sessions with various producers, "Don't Tell Me" became the front-runner to be the lead single, and the label's stance on Walker as cowriter softened. Walker didn't tell me which parts of "Don't Tell Me" he wrote and which parts Lavigne held the pen for, but there's a line about kicking ass in there, and I bet that was hers. This woman *loves* to talk about kicking ass.

Walker went back out to LA for some final sessions with Avril as the album was being finalized. Sitting at his hotel bar the night before they were meeting up, Walker scribbled out an idea for a piano ballad on a cocktail napkin. It was dark and twisty, with a chorus full of verbose wordplay. He played it for Lavigne the next day in studio and she loved the song, but when he got to the chorus he thought was clever, she cocked her head to the side in confusion. "I don't get it," she told him. "I had a real awakening thinking, that's probably ten million young girls cocking their heads at the same time and saying in unison, 'We don't get it,' " Walker said.

They simplified the chorus together, landing on something direct and potent:

> *All this time you were pretending / so much for my happy*
> *ending*

"Don't Tell Me" and "My Happy Ending" became the first and second singles off *Under My Skin*. This, it seemed, was who Lavigne wanted to be, still radio friendly but harder. She leaned into punk rock history on her tour—called the "Bonez Tour," where Walker opened for her in several locations and where he and Taubenfeld would frequently share music with her. "We would play her T-Rex and stuff like that," Walker said.

This was as punk as Lavigne would ever get. "Don't Tell Me" went to number twenty-two and "My Happy Ending" was a top-ten hit, peaking at number nine for four weeks in June 2004. At one point, Simple Plan and Blink-182 were opening for her. But there was no "Complicated" on *Under My Skin* and the album as a whole, though successful, sold less than half of what *Let Go* had two years prior. A huge amount of the album's promotion was centered around proving that Lavigne was her own writer, which put the emphasis on something that wasn't her ultimate strength. For an artist credited with tapping into something authentic, Lavigne can be hard to locate in her songs—her voice is distinct, but it doesn't convey a lot of emotion, and even her songs that tell a story with a narrative arc don't rely on rich detail. Sometimes, this is the magic—if Lavigne ever gave us the actual answer to what made things so complicated, it might become a song about her instead of a song about everyone. If she sang in a way that emphasized certain plot points of "Sk8er Boi" above others, it might highlight the discrepancies between the kiss-off quality to the song and the fact that, within it, Lavigne ends up with everything she wants. You could call the ability to do this being an excellent pop star, but Lavigne was not too keen on doing so at the time.

Critics had challenged Lavigne to express her own perspective after *Let Go,* but they turned out not to find what she had to say terribly interesting. Even a positive *Rolling Stone* review noted that the music and Lavigne's delivery covered up some lyrical vacuousness; a scathing write-up in *The Guardian* claimed that "the music is so anodyne that you don't pay much attention to Lavigne's lyrics," which "proves to be a small mercy." *Under My Skin* was by no means a failure, and from everything I know it's the album Lavigne wanted to make, but you could see where she might have felt she was in a no-win situation, called out for not having written the songs people loved the most, then taking firmer grasp of the pen only to be told she wasn't a good enough lyricist.

Lavigne took a few years off from recording and married Sum 41 front man Deryck Whibley. Then she dyed her hair platinum blond. We should have known.

The next time the world heard from Avril Lavigne was three years later, in 2007. It was jarring. First of all, she was screaming: *Hey! Hey! You! You! I don't like your girlfrannnnnnd!* Second of all, she was wearing pink. Like, hot pink. Blond Avril was . . . different. One of the hallmark differentiators between Lavigne and her bubblegum pop predecessors had been the fact that she didn't work with Max Martin. But for the first single of her third album *The Best Damn Thing,* she went to one of his main protégés, Lukasz Gottwald, a.k.a. Dr. Luke. You're going to hear a lot about Luke later, much of it bad, but the important thing to understand at this point is that he was Martin's main collaborator. They'd met when Luke was the lead guitarist for *Saturday Night Live*'s house band while also DJing in clubs around town, which was where the two of them connected. Their first real project together was Kelly Clarkson's "Since U Been Gone," which had netted Martin his first top-ten hit in four years. Luke was a hot name, but by working with him, it was as if Lavigne was giving up on her quest for hardcore credibility. Sid Vicious would not have worked with Dr. Luke.

"Girlfriend" is almost like a parody of a pop song. I don't want to say that there's nothing "real" about the song; it seems real enough to me that there's some guy and Avril Lavigne doesn't like his girlfriend. But it's total empty calories. The lyrics are sublimely dumb, in that they are mostly just *hey hey you you I don't like your girlfriend!* The melody is irrelevant, the point of the song is for Avril Lavigne to yell *hey hey you you I don't like your girlfriend* and for you to yell that along with her. It has no substance, and that's intentional. Lavigne said she wrote the song in two minutes while drunk, and in the bridge you can even hear her and Luke cackling in the background of the recording. It's fun. I like it, and so did a lot of other people, because it became both Lavigne's and Luke's first number one.

For the record, some questions surrounding authorship emerged regarding "Girlfriend," too. (This happens to Avril Lavigne a lot, but it happens to Dr. Luke *a lot* a lot.) The band the Rubinoos wound up suing Lavigne and Luke, claiming that they'd ripped the lyrics from their 1979 single "I Wanna Be Your Boyfriend." Lavigne and Luke denied the charges and Lavigne was very upset. On Myspace, she posted a long and spicy statement beginning thusly:

"You may have heard some news that two guys who wrote for some band from the 1970s I have never in my life heard of called the 'Rubinoos' (quotations hers) are trying to sue me," Lavigne wrote. She has always dealt a good burn.

The Rubinoos didn't seem to have an awesome claim. The words are really basic, and "Girlfriend" reminds me a lot more of "Mickey" by Toni Basil than the song that, like Lavigne, I had not heard before this came up. Everyone wound up settling out of court, which annoyed Lavigne, but she put it all behind her. No one really cared, anyway. Lavigne had gone pop, so the old purity tests no longer applied. She seemed to preempt potential critiques that *The Best Damn Thing* wasn't real enough or punk enough or singer-songwriter-y enough by dismissing the premise, too. And she wound up sounding a lot like she didn't care about her own album. "Some of the songs I wrote didn't even mean that much to me," Lavigne wrote on her blog. "It's not like some personal thing I'm going through. They're just songs."

Lavigne's career got pretty weird after that. She had a couple more hits—having already broken the seal in working with Dr. Luke,

Lavigne went to Max Martin himself for the lead single of her 2011 record *Goodbye Lullaby,* "What the Hell." "Here's to Never Growing Up," which kicked off her self-titled 2013 album, was similar party-all-night Top 40 bait (but pretty good, and Lavigne says "kiss my ass" a lot in the chorus, and it's always good when Lavigne is saying "ass" in songs). But her records as a whole declined in popularity. She veered strangely into Japanese iconography, releasing a song called "Hello Kitty" also on *Avril Lavigne* that got her some extremely well-deserved accusations of appropriation including for the moment in which she randomly yells "Kawaii!" over, um, dubstep. (A few years ago, I went to an Avril Lavigne show on a whim, and was deeply weirded out to find that half the audience was young people in Hello Kitty costumes.) In 2014, she contracted Lyme disease, which nearly killed her and had her on bed rest for five months, exacerbated by several initial misdiagnoses as chronic fatigue. It was also during this time that her second marriage, to Nickelback front man Chad Kroeger ended, and Lavigne mostly retreated from public life.

In 2011, a Brazilian blog called *Avril Esta Morta* went online. It posited that Lavigne had died by suicide in 2003 and had been replaced by a body double named Melissa Vandella. That idea had been bandied about on the internet since around 2005, right around the time that Lavigne had started changing up her look ahead of "Girlfriend." The blog, though, laid the theory out convincingly enough for a following to coalesce around it. Melissa, it went, was originally hired to help keep the press off Avril's trail. The two became close—IRL, Avril once did a photo shoot with the name Melissa written on her hand. After the release of *Let Go,* though, Avril struggled with the pressures of fame and the death of her grandfather and fell into a deep depression. When she eventually took her own life, the industrial complex around her as a star was too big to fail, so Melissa was convinced to play Avril for appearances. "Rich people and influential people are capable of setting up anything, and hiding anything too! It's hard to say how many people could be involved in this, but it wouldn't be difficult to hide her death as there would be a perfect replacement," the blog reads. Evidence of the change was found in the way she dresses (Avril wears cargo pants, Melissa wears dresses) and in the shape of her nose (can't think of any other reason that might change!). Side-by-side photos of the crinkles in the corners of her eyelids were compared and contrasted, handwriting analysis was done. Notably, fan theorists latched on to the idea that the real Avril never would have "gone pop." A post on the original message board cites how dramatic the shift to "Girlfriend" was. A Twitter thread from 2017 with 143,000 retweets uses a comparison of "Complicated" to "Hello Kitty" as its first point of evidence.

The thing was, it was a bit. The blog was one of a few similar celebrity-death-hoax blogs created to see if they could get traction, the end goal being to display how easy it was to get people to buy into conspiracy theories. There was one for Selena Gomez and another for Paul McCartney. There *was* text on the site divulging it as a social experiment, but only in Portuguese. But internet's gonna internet, and the rumor spread. Websites like AvrilLavigneDied.blogspot.com were created. A YouTuber going by "Avril may be dead" uploaded several minutes of what she called video evidence, which was mostly just pictures of Lavigne's nose from different angles. Users on the conspiracy forum Godlike Productions started posting about the replacement theory. Believers named themselves the "Avril Rangers," and started posting their evidence on music message boards. There were twists and turns. On the site ATRL.net, a user called Vulps posted a photo of "Avr1l"—Ranger-speak for the original Lavigne—buying cheese when the new Avril had claimed to have cut out dairy. Missing wrist tattoos apparently confirmed that this could not be Melissa. "So could it be?" Vulps wrote. "Is the original Avril Lavigne still alive and well? And if so, why did she construct such an elaborate lie to deceive her fans? Was it because we didn't take Complicated to number one? The Grammy losses to Norah Jones?? Or did her record label have a part to play in this?"

The theory bubbled up through the 2010s and eventually became mainstream enough to reach Lavigne. At the time, no one knew she had actually been fighting for her life so recently, which puts her frustration when confronted with it into context. "It's just a dumb internet rumor and I'm flabbergasted that people bought into it," Lavigne told EW in 2019. "Isn't that so weird? It's so dumb, and I look the exact same. On one hand, everyone is like 'Oh my God, you look the same,' and on the other hand people are like 'Oh my God, she died.'"

In 2015, a Facebook user claiming to be the author of the original blog tried to correct the record. "The blog was a way of showing how conspiracy theories may seem true. Many people believe everything they see on the internet, but is this really right? . . . I created this theory to see if people would believe, and thousands of people believed that this was a fact." The user went on to note that they hadn't invented any of the supposed evidence for the theory, demonstrating how conspiracies can be pulled out of real life without much fabrication. "I apologize for the people who believed she was dead and feel disappointed by this revelation, but it was for you to become more suspicious people and do not believe everything you see!"

Of course, many of the readers of the post were not ready to hear this. They had already decided. "Explain how she changed her height," one wrote. "And the timbre of her voice changed." It was too late to put the theory back in its box; Avril Lavigne's internet footprint became inextricably linked with conspiracy. In 2017, the malware expert McAfee named *Avril Lavigne* "the most dangerous celebrity search term" on the internet, a.k.a. the one that was most likely to generate results that were malware scams leading to scam websites and cybercrime traps.

The Avril Lavigne death hoax was built, primarily, on the randomness of the web. But I can't help but think it wasn't a total coincidence that hers was the one that stuck, not Selena Gomez's or Paul McCartney's. Fraudulence has always been a thorn in her side. There's an irony to that in the sense that Avril Lavigne's career is actually remarkably consistent in what she does well, which is to sing hooky, punk-tinged pop songs in her piercing yelp or rowdy snarl. But her career was less often viewed as being about what she was than what she wasn't, be that Britney, a true punk, or even alive.

Since then, I think our obsession with "authenticity" in music has waned, or we've at least become a little wiser in how we determine what's real and what's phony. Lavigne's early career is set against the backdrop of . . . *Baby One More Time* as a reaction to teen pop, and the punky textures she added to Top 40 made her a headliner in the second major wave of 2000s pop after Britney and co's dance-pop opening chapters. But when it came to actually placing her *within* a musical lineage, Lavigne found herself being asked to live up to a set of rock-oriented standards that were a poor fit for her. As one of the first pop stars of the aughts to play with punk and rock aesthetics that recalled the most heralded music of the nineties, the twists, turns, and dramas that followed Lavigne's breakout revealed the limits of applying rock standards to pop music.

In Lavigne's time, a major conversation about the hierarchy of genre—why rockers are the ones to set the terms of the test in the first place—was imminent, but a moment too late for her to fully benefit from. But that conversation may never have taken place if she hadn't laid such a clear example of why it was needed—and set the stage for the artist who actually did spark the debate that would help future artists following in Lavigne's pop-punk footsteps earn the respect they deserved.

4

In Defense of
Ashlee Simpson

IF THE TRIALS AND COMPLICATIONS OF AVRIL LAVIGNE, punk rock princess, could not have made it any more obvious that pop needed something to pull it out of the shadow of rock 'n' roll, it was one of her musical offspring that sparked a critical conversation about making that happen. Let's go now to Studio 8H at 30 Rockefeller Plaza in New York City on the night of October 23, 2004.

On this night, a very blond Jude Law was hosting *Saturday Night Live* in the middle of his promotion cycle for *Alfie*. Law was pretty good; at various times he played Tony Blair, Nicky Hilton, and Mr. Rochester from *Jane Eyre*, who in the world of the sketch, kept Rachel Dratch as a booty call locked in his attic. The range! Everything was going well until around 12:45 a.m. ET, when Law turned to the camera and uttered four of the least likely words to have altered the course of pop history: "Once again, Ashlee Simpson."

Simpson, the musical guest, was enjoying a victory lap promoting her debut album *Autobiography* and her new MTV reality show *The Ashlee Simpson Show*. Earlier in the evening, she'd performed her single "Pieces of Me" without incident. After Law's introduction, she took the stage in her best Warped Tour chic: tartan plaid sweater-vest, cargo pants held low around her hips by a studded belt and various chains, and Hot Topic accoutrements hanging via carabiner from her pant loops. She was flanked by her band and back out to perform her album's title track.

Then, disaster. The band began playing "Autobiography," to which Ashlee gyrated weirdly with her hands in the air. This was actually not the disaster. That came just after the intro, when the audience began to hear the vocal for "Pieces of Me," but Ashlee wasn't singing it. Credit to the band for responding flawlessly, they transitioned quickly into "Pieces of Me." But Simpson wasn't so composed. She stood on the stage for a few moments, looked around, then started dancing a funny little jig. She kept it up for about thirty seconds, then walked offstage. The band, who go down in history as the only people to handle this situation remotely well, kept playing. After way too long, someone in the control room figured out that they should get out of this and jumped to commercial after airing a promo card of Jude Law's face.

Simpson had been caught lip-synching. She'd later claim to have had either a sore throat or vocal lesions that had caused a doctor to tell her not to sing that night. But no one could get their stories straight. Geffen Records said there was merely a mix-up between a prerecorded drum track and the vocal, and that someone had pressed the wrong button. Either way, Simpson had been exposed. She returned at the end of the show, standing next to a grinning Law, looking sheepish. "I feel so bad," she said to camera. "My band started playing the wrong song, and I didn't know what to do, so I thought I'd do a hoedown. I'm sorry. It's live TV. Things happen. I'm sorry."

The dynamics around Simpson being exposed as a lip-syncher were similar to those around Lavigne being accused of getting more songwriting help than she claimed, in large part because Ashlee Simpson was an artist in the Avril Lavigne mold. Just as Britney begat a dozen Christinas, Jessicas, and Mandys, Lavigne's success in the wake of *Let Go* led to a rush by many labels to find other young female artists who could capitalize on the same pop-punk trend.

Scott Spock, one of the producers from the Matrix, told me that after 2002 he was getting regular calls from labels asking if he could make another "Complicated." That was ultimately how they wound up working with Hilary Duff on *Metamorphosis*, and with the Canadian girl band Lillix, whose 2003 debut *Falling Uphill* included the single "It's About Time" and the "What I Like About You" cover that featured on the *Freaky Friday* soundtrack. Artists like Fefe Dobson, Skye Sweetnam, and Aly & AJ, who conjured Avril comparisons, also got opportunities. Remember the Veronicas? The Australian twin sister duo with semi-edgy pop bangers like "4ever," "Everything I'm Not," and "Untouched," are a good example of how much development support a group that checked those boxes could get at the time. For their first album, label Sire Records paired the sisters, Lisa and Jessica Origliasso, with songwriters who had or would go on to write Gwen Stefani's "Rich Girl" and Christina Aguilera's "Ain't No Other Man" (Kara DioGuardi), John Legend's "All of Me" and Beyoncé's "If I Were a Boy" (Toby Gad), Cyndi Lauper's "True Colors" and Madonna's "Like a Virgin" (Billy Steinberg), *and* Max Martin, who brought Dr. Luke and Rami Yacoub with him. Go back and turn on that Veronicas record right now, you won't be disappointed. Those songs sound *expensive*.

Because these women were often toeing the same line between pop and rock that Lavigne did, they were vulnerable to similar critiques of whether they were "authentic" artists or just vessels in search of a hit. When indie artist Liz Phair worked with the Matrix on "Why Can't I?," the biggest hit of her career, *The New York Times* headlined its negative review: "Exile in Avril-ville," a riff on Phair's debut album, *Exile in Guyville* (itself a reference to the Rolling Stones' *Exile on Main Street*). "Not only will Ms. Phair alienate her old fan base, as she has defensively acknowledged in recent interviews, but in trying to remodel herself as a contemporary Avril Lavigne or Alanis Morissette, she's revealed herself to be astonishingly tone-deaf to her own strengths," the review claimed. Like they had in Lavigne's case, these criticisms revealed the limitations of assessing a pop song as if it was striving to be something more alternative rather than meeting it on its own terms. (They also revealed the limits of not hearing that "Why Can't I?" is a ridiculously good song, but that's for another day.) These double standards that cast women as sellouts for making music people liked were there for anyone paying close attention but they mostly remained as subtext until Law's fateful intro: "Once again, Ashlee Simpson. . . ."

Ashlee was the most obvious Avril descendant. Like Avril, she had a pure pop foil—in Ashlee's case her older sister Jessica, a blond Texan church crooner at heart who'd become pop royalty by virtue of her relationship with Nick Lachey and their MTV reality show *Newlyweds: Nick & Jessica*. It wasn't terribly clear, when she signed her record deal with Geffen in 2003, whether Simpson wanted to be a pop star or merely famous—she'd recorded a song for the *Freaky Friday* soundtrack, done some acting, and guested as a veejay on *TRL*. But she had a gravelly quality to her voice, was comparatively edgy compared to her sister, and had recently dyed her naturally blond hair dark brown—so pop punk it was. For her debut album in 2004, Ashlee, her overzealous showbiz dad Joe, and her managers tapped two of the best pop-punk hitmakers working at the time, John Shanks and Kara DioGuardi, who packed the album full of bubble-grunge guitar riffs, earworm melodies, and faux emo non sequiturs like *Got stains on my T-shirt / And I'm the biggest flirt.* Their choice for the album title nodded to the singer-songwriter lane Simpson was positioning herself in: *Autobiography.* The lead single, "Pieces of Me," an ode to Simpson's then boyfriend—say it with me: Ryan Cabrera—with a perfect sing-along chorus, reached number five on the Hot 100 and helped *Autobiography* go triple platinum and become 2004's biggest debut by a female artist.

Still, standing on the *SNL* stage, backed by a live band, in Doc Martens à la Pete Townshend, it was easy to look at Simpson and see someone playing dress-up instead of a real artist. This was always the trapdoor for pop rockers like Simpson—rock worships "realness" and "authenticity" as ideals, while pop almost always involves some element of fantasy or fabrication. Simpson was tsk-tsked by *SNL* overlord Lorne Michaels, who said he hadn't approved the use of the backing track and that it went against the show's live essence. In a stroke of bad luck, the *SNL* process was being featured on that week's *60 Minutes,* so several other crew members also spoke to how shocked they were by Simpson's lack of preparedness. In *The Washington Post,* the incident was compared to Janet Jackson's wardrobe snafu at the Super Bowl earlier that year. Three months after *SNL,* Simpson gave a shaky performance of "La La" at the Orange Bowl and was met with boos. "Pulling an Ashlee Simpson" became synonymous with being exposed during a live performance.

A week after the *SNL* incident, *The New York Times* music critic Kelefa Sanneh published a piece under the headline, "The Rap

Against Rockism." In it, Sanneh argued that Simpson's fall from grace was not evidence of her own artistic or musical failure, but of prejudices in music criticism that were becoming increasingly out of tune with the way popular music was created and consumed. He summed up those prejudices in one term: "rockism." The term wasn't Sanneh's invention—it was in use among music obsessives in the United Kingdom at least since the eighties—but his essay marked its entrance into the mainstream. And if rockism, as Sanneh described it, made rock 'n' roll the standard-bearer for all music only to weaponize those standards against anything that wasn't rebellious, guitar-based, or album-centric enough, it certainly seemed like a useful lens through which to consider someone like Simpson. "Countless critics assail pop stars for not being rock 'n' roll enough, without stopping to wonder why that should be everybody's goal," Sanneh wrote.

"The Rap Against Rockism" was a massively influential piece of writing. Though Sanneh never actually used this word, his essay became the manifesto of a new, or at least newly articulated, ideology of music criticism called poptimism. Poptimism argued that pop music was just as worthy of serious critical attention as rock 'n' roll or anything else, and that it deserved to be considered on its own terms—if a song is trying to make people dance, or to be a radio hit, then it should be assessed for how successful it is in doing those things, not for how closely it hews to the image of Led Zeppelin playing Budokan.

It was a worthwhile correction—critics' disproportionate focus on rock not only set up pop stars like Simpson or Lavigne, who had rockish sensibilities for failure, but had led many to miss the fact that, if music had a defining genre coming out of the nineties, it was hip-hop, not indie or alternative rock. It was easy to get on board with poptimism, then, because it was useful. It had a righteous quality, too, since it tended to celebrate the contributions of Black and female artists who were often overlooked by rock 'n' roll evangelists. Poptimism did not become criticism's default point of view overnight after Simpson's snafu or Sanneh's essay—an oft-cited piece of evidence that rockism did not go quietly is the fact that the music tastemaker publication *Pitchfork* did not review a Taylor Swift album until *Reputation* in 2016, despite having reviewed indie rocker Ryan Adams's cover version of her *1989* in 2015. Still, the ideas proved sticky. By the end of the decade, especially around and after a particularly dominant stretch of pure pop in the early 2010s by stars like Katy Perry, Lady Gaga, and Swift, poptimism was no longer provocative but intuitive.

Despite being its catalyst, Ashlee Simpson did not really remain the face of the poptimist debate. Her career didn't last long enough to see it through to the 2010s when it became clear that the poptimists had won. Simpson got a redo on *SNL* in 2005, a year after her infamous performance, which went much better, but the shine was still off her star. Her sophomore record *I Am Me* didn't get to a million in sales and her days of real relevance on the pop scene were over. Pop punk was going out of vogue, anyway—the pop-rock sensibility that made her a good subject for a conversation about why rock *shouldn't* be the genre all others were held up against actually made her a poor fit once that debate made the leap to one about why pop *was* worthy of that role, since the most interesting pop music in the mid-aughts tended to come from rap and R&B spaces.

Ashlee didn't beat the charges that she was phony, either. In 2006, she covered an issue of *Marie Claire,* preaching self-acceptance and positive body image. But soon after the interview and photo shoot, she got a nose job, which led to some genuine public outrage. "She was quoting chapter and verse about how crucial it is to love yourself as you are, etc.," Editor-in-Chief Joanna Coles wrote in the following issue, where she addressed various angry letters to the editor over Simpson's betrayal. Quickly, more fell apart for the Simpson clan writ large. Jessica and Nick Lachey divorced, after which she started dating Dallas Cowboys quarterback Tony Romo. When he played poorly, she was nicknamed Yoko Romo. Jessica eventually rebounded selling shoes and fragrances under the Jessica Simpson Collection label, and Ashlee has had further forays into reality TV with her now-husband Evan Ross, son of Diana. But the Simpson dynasty was over, its run ultimately short-lived. And looking back at the timeline, the *SNL* snafu started the decline.

Still, if Ashlee Simpson needs to fill the role of poptimist icon, the poptimists could do worse. A core tenet of poptimism is that it accepts the mechanics of stardom, the elaborate, often corporate machines that help pop stars sell fantasy. *Autobiography* is a pretty good testament to the capacity of that machine—a forty-three-minute album by a woman with middling interest in music and the best producers money could buy, that happens to be really, really good.

If *Autobiography* was a testament to pop hitmaking, the Simpsons, reality TV presence was another piece of mid-aughts culture that influenced our collective understanding of the constructed nature of celebrity. As a famous family, they started out offering an unvarnished look at themselves; *Newlyweds* entered the zeitgeist with Jessica asking Nick Lachey if her can of tuna was chicken or fish. Remember: These were the early days of reality TV, when getting an inside look at those gaffes really did seem genuine, at least in contrast to *Vogue* profiles with airbrushed cover shots. But eventually, after breakups and surgeries, and once reality audiences became more aware of the editing and production choices that shape unscripted shows, audiences began to better understand and accept that we are always being at least a little bit manipulated by our entertainers. That may be the Simpsons' truest legacy, as a famous family that helped teach us that stars are almost always performing on some level. A lot of these "scandals" feel quaint now; it's hard to imagine impassioned letters to the editor of *Marie Claire* today about a nose job. Plastic surgery may still be easy gossip fodder, but I think these days we all understand that most famous people—and a lot of normies, too—are walking around with some replacement parts out there. Ashlee Simpson's nose job was just before its time.

As for poptimism itself, the fact that it has become the dominant mode of ideology in our musical discourse is one of the most lasting imprints of 2000s pop, and one of the clearest means by which attitudes toward pop music and pop stars have been transformed. The best form of the poptimist argument, and the closest to what Sanneh wrote when he argued not *for* poptimism but *against* rockism, was that music should be evaluated on its own terms and no genre should be taken as inherently more interesting or valuable than another. This was not only useful for disentangling the critical obsession with indie and alt-rock from discourse around other music but also for keeping up with the way listeners were hearing and discovering music thanks to changes in technology. If poptimism became a mainstream idea in the early aughts, its rise coincided with the start of the MP3 era, which reduced the number of barriers a listener faced when trying to hear a lot of different kinds of music. It also devalued the album in favor of the single, given that individual songs were easier and easier to come by, which undermined a core rockist principle, that the album reigned supreme.

MP3s, in general, fit with poptimist principles because they favored popularity on something like the iTunes Store chart over affinity. Genres sort music into various lineages based on musical signifiers, like banjos in country or 808 drums in hip-hop, but their most practical purpose in the CD era was a commercial one—telling consumers which bins in a record store to sort through to find the things they liked. As the marketplace changed in ways that made it easier to find and discover new music, genre itself became less important and more fluid than it used to be. In 2004, the year of Ashlee's *SNL* snafu, Britney Spears was singing pop music while Usher was doing R&B, but they were working with the same producers and for similar audiences. This was the benefit of poptimist thinking—it didn't ask what box those songs belonged in, it merely asked if they were good.

There is a thornier side of the poptimist legacy, though. Sanneh's essay advocated only for ditching the music industry's bias toward rock, but over time, poptimism has developed a tendency to replace that bias with another one, toward what is *popular*. I think there's value, when something is widely enjoyed, in trying to understand what those audiences are hearing and responding to. But popularity does not automatically mean quality, which some iterations of poptimism, particularly when coupled with the activist impulses of stan culture, seem to imply. In a 2015 essay, *The Washington Post*'s Chris Richards wrote that poptimism was "becoming worshipful of fame" and that "it treats megastars, despite their untold corporate resources, like underdogs." Richards continued, "It grants immunity to a lot of dim music. Worst of all, it asks everyone to agree on the winners and then cheer louder."

I think there's some truth to that, though I think what Richards is describing has more to do with stan culture—and stan groups claiming to act under the *banner* of poptimism when they fight for artists who are already winning—than it does with the actual ideas behind poptimism. Poptimism shouldn't ask listeners to agree on the winners, but I don't think its fundamental instinct to engage with music that's broadly popular is pointing it toward bad music.

Perhaps this is the right time to acknowledge that Ashlee Simpson in 2004 could *absolutely win an argument on the merits of her album.* The summer I turned twenty-one, I was living in Washington, D.C., where I went to college, and had a bunch of friends from different parts of my life come stay with me and go to a party I was throwing in my apartment. The party was intended to be small, but I'd thrown a Facebook invitation to a guy in my class I had a massive, raging crush on, and when he actually accepted it—despite the fact that I didn't know if it was a real RSVP or just a courtesy one—I felt the need to make it a bigger deal. This led to another round of Facebook invites and the ordering of a keg and Party City decorations, which meant that by the day of, what had been planned as a small get-together was a full-on event, and I had a lot of setting up to do. This was complicated by the fact that a half-dozen or so out-of-towners were rolling in throughout the day, arriving to an undecorated apartment and a frantic host, sweaty from wrangling a keg in and out of an Uber and into the building. By the middle of the afternoon, I was still organizing while my guests stood around in the living room.

Somewhere, amid my harried energy, the awkwardness of just standing around and the tendency of small talk to devolve into an exercise in proving how well you're doing, and what a cool internship you had, and *oh, you went to Paris last month? I'm going next week,* things got weirdly tense. It wasn't anyone's fault, the vibes were just off and people needed something to do. It was in that moment, in a stroke of genuine genius I will never forget, that my friend Eliana located the aux cord to my speakers, plugged her phone in, and put on "Pieces of Me." In a matter of one chorus, everyone went from sizing each other up to singing in unison. I don't think anybody in my living room that night was thinking about *SNL,* and if they were, it was a nostalgic memory, not an indictment. If a key part of poptimism is moving on from outdated genre hierarchies that act like only certain types of artists are important enough to last, I think the way everyone came together over a fifteen-year-old song represents that well.

In this century's arc of pop stardom, there is probably no singular shift more important to the rising status of the pop star than the introduction of poptimism as a counterargument to rockism. We live in a world rich with writing about artists like Taylor Swift, where a pop star like Rihanna can perform with shredding electric guitars and be lauded for it, and where a new pop punk like Olivia Rodrigo doesn't have to worry so much about how she fits in a particular genre box. All this, and our growing awareness that there's some sleight of hand at work in all entertainment, has been for the better. Ashlee Simpson didn't bungle *SNL* on the merits of her artistry, she bungled it by an old set of standards that set her up to fail. But thankfully, the right people recognized this and wound up starting one of the most impactful conversations on how music is covered, one that now helps so many pop stars get their due.

5

Beyoncé Before Beyoncé

"HISTORY IN THE MAKING," JAY-Z SAID.

It was the spring of 2003. Jay, king of the New York rap scene at the time, had shown up to the studio to record the intro to Beyoncé's "Crazy in Love." He sounded almost as if he couldn't believe it. *"So crazy right now!"* A notorious bachelor, heeding a call to come to Midtown on a few hours' notice and simp into a microphone over his future wife. *"Most incredibly! It's your girl, B!"*

Now that is down *bad*.

Everything about the "Crazy in Love" intro is perfectly rendered to let you know that what's about to happen is a Big Fucking Deal. There's Jay's presence in and of itself. There's the genuine glee in his delivery. There is literal fanfare—the horn section is a sample of Chicago soul quartet the Chi-Lites' "Are You My Woman? (Tell Me So)," and it's there to tell you to pay attention. A queen is coming. Uh-oh, uh-oh . . .

There is some irony to the fact that, around this same time, artists like Avril Lavigne and Ashlee Simpson were becoming symbols of a debate over genre-based biases in popular music. That conversation was more than necessary, and the fact that it revolved largely around artists who blurred the lines between pop and rock made sense considering the stranglehold that rock in particular had on the music industry writ large. But if an aim of poptimism was to celebrate the most exciting music of the moment (instead of holding it up against old ideals), the irony was that most of that music sounded very little like Ashlee Simpson and a lot more like "Crazy in Love."

In 2015, researchers at Imperial College London published an influential research paper on the most significant moments in popular music history. The study drew attention because it argued that 1991—the year N.W.A's *Niggaz4Life* became the first album by a rap group to top the *Billboard* 200 and seeded an explosion of rap and hip-hop into mainstream culture—marked the single most impactful shift in the evolution of popular music.

The research was done using a digital analysis of chord progressions, tonal shifts, rhythm, and other sonic elements (but no lyrics) using more than seventeen thousand songs, the vast majority of the tracks that had charted on the *Billboard* Hot 100 in the United States between 1960 and 2010. They ignored any pre-assessments of genre, searching not for aesthetics but for the underlying structure of how songs are made. For example, the frequency of the dominant seventh chord, common in jazz and blues, declined by about 75 percent between 1960 and 2009, reflecting the diminished presence of those genres on the charts. The research team was searching for watershed moments where fundamental changes took place, then stuck, and found three big ones: the British Invasion of 1964, the synth-pop revolution circa 1983, and 1991.

What happened in '91 had less to do with how popularity was

achieved than how it was *observed*. N.W.A topping the charts coincided with the release of Nielsen SoundScan, a consumer report
collected using point-of-sales data from cash registers at record
stores that replaced the practice of stores self-reporting their sales.
SoundScan was put into use around the same time that *Billboard*
switched from trusting radio stations' self-reports to using a third-
party service to monitor airplay. The effect was that for the first
time, the charts were actual statistical reflections of what music
Americans were buying and listening to. What that reflection
showed was hard evidence of a massive interest in hip-hop—and
that concrete data gave artists in the genre a boost of tangible power
within the music industry.

The surprise of those research findings was how significant that
boost was. The Beatles' release of "I Want to Hold Your Hand" in
the US on December 26, 1963, is oft-cited as *the* man-walks-on-
hind-legs event of popular music history, but the authors of the
study claimed that the hip-hop revolution was even more significant. The beginning of an era when the sounds, structures, and
producers of hip-hop would influence other genres, from dance to
country, and become the underlying sound of modern popular
music, marked "the single most important event that has shaped
the musical structure of the American charts," the authors wrote.
History in the making, indeed.

By the early 2000s, a decade-plus after that watershed moment
in 1991, these shifts were baked into the *Billboard* charts. In the
most mainstream musical formats, the sounds of hip-hop and
R&B—essential sounds to the artistic legacy of Black Americans—
had become the default setting. On October 11, 2003, for the first
time ever, the entire top ten of the Hot 100 was occupied by Black
artists. But while pop *music* clearly reflected this reality, pop *stardom* did not. The echelon of artists who were cover girls for major

magazines, the kind whose celebrity appeal existed symbiotically with their music, remained overwhelmingly white. But in her breakout years as a solo artist, Beyoncé broke through these barriers by synthesizing the sounds of hip-hop and R&B with the narrative appeal—largely built around her relationship with Jay-Z—of an A-list pop star, and therefore widened the definition of what a pop star could look and sound like.

By the time Beyoncé was plotting her solo debut, hip-hop had not only gained recognition as one of the most *popular* musical formats, it had also developed a symbiotic relationship with *pop* music. (*Niggaz4Life* was a hugely popular album, but N.W.A was not making pop songs.) Musically, there was one critical vehicle for this crossover to mainstream audiences (usually a euphemism for white audiences) to take place: the R&B hook. Sugarhill Gang's "Rapper's Delight" from 1979 is often cited as the first mainstream crossover record by a hip-hop group, and that song is built on the baseline of Chic's "Good Times." A hook like that gave a song based otherwise in rap verses and a beat the kind of melody a pop audience could latch on to. By the 1990s, recording technology had made that kind of musical cutting and pasting easier for producers, and the rise of hip-hop coincided with this period when heavy sampling, particularly of those R&B hooks that lent melody, was possible and common.

Sampling, though, could be costly. Throughout the nineties, sample-happy producers like Dr. Dre or Rick Rubin often found themselves cutting big checks to the artists they borrowed from or dealing with lawsuits and criticism. To avoid this, up-and-coming producers like Swizz Beatz and Timbaland, in their early careers, tried to avoid sampling whenever possible. One upshot of this was that from the midnineties heading into the aughts, hip-hop-fluent artists who could sing their own hooks came to make up a growing portion of the pop landscape. This group included artists like Mary J. Blige or Usher, who crooned over the mechanized 808 drums and hi hats popularized by Southern rappers. The duo of Ashanti and Ja Rule offered both pieces of the puzzle—Ja on the beats and Ashanti with the hooks.

It is hard to imagine how this music could have been any more mainstream than it was. In the mid-aughts, I was a middle schooler at a Vermont day school that was probably 90 percent white, and Lil Jon was a defining sound of my school dances. I wish I could tell you I have no memories of a couple dozen twelve-year-olds screeching "Get Low" in unison in the meeting room of a local town hall, but what I must instead admit is that they exist, and they are vivid as the day is long. We were not alone in our appropriations—it was also around this time that many white artists from pure pop backgrounds started incorporating hip-hop sounds and producers into their work. Britney Spears, who'd gotten famous singing songs out of Max Martin's Swedish hit factory, started spending a lot of studio time in Virginia Beach where the Neptunes were mixing hits, including "I'm a Slave 4 U," the lead single of her third album, *Britney*. Meanwhile, her ex-boyfriend (and future Notes App apologist) Justin Timberlake was busy getting Timbaland to write his diss tracks, which was not the first time he'd been a little too comfortable adopting rappers' trappings as his own. One of the most hilarious and memorable excerpts of Spears's recent memoir, *The Woman in Me*, was a story about Timberlake saying the phrase "fo shiz" over and over in an attempt to impress Ginuwine.

Any glance at the charts or spin on a radio dial at the time made it pretty obvious that hip-hop was pop. And yet in the world of mainstream *celebrity*, the image of pop stardom painted by the glossy magazine covers in the grocery checkout aisle was still both starkly white and largely ignorant of the genres that had overtaken

music. Between 1990 and 2004, just nine Latinas or Black women—
Neneh Cherry, Whitney Houston, Janet Jackson, Mariah Carey,
Lauryn Hill, Christina Aguilera, Jennifer Lopez, Alicia Keys, and
Shakira received solo features on the cover of *Rolling Stone*; Jerry
Seinfeld alone had three, plus a cast photo. The tabloids and glossy
mags were, if anything, worse—in that same period, the only Black
woman in music to cover *Vogue* was Mel B in the Spice Girls' January 1998 feature. While there was a clear relationship between the
interest in an artist like Britney Spears's life and the interest in her
music, that feedback loop did not exist for a lot of Black artists,
which meant that hip-hop could dominate popular music while
being shut out of the elite celebrity spaces that promote true pop
stardom.

What caused this? The obvious answer is also the right one—it
was mostly just straight-up racism. Celebrity media in general was
blindingly white at this time; a 2017 study from Stanford's journalism project found that only 12 percent of *Vogue* cover subjects from
1990 to 2017 were Black or Latino; in *Harper's Bazaar* the figure
was only 8 percent. Remember—this encompassed years like 2004,
when all thirteen of the songs that hit number one on the Hot 100
were performed by Black artists. If true stardom is a balancing act
between staying on top of the trends defining culture while captur-
ing some rarefied timeless quality, the goalposts always seemed to
be moving on Black female artists in one of those two directions.

The most of-the-moment artists often seemed to be pigeonholed
by genre, even by their own advocates. The disgraced former Up-
town Records executive Sean Combs, who at the time went by
Puffy, nicknamed Blige the Queen of Hip-Hop Soul as part of promoting her. A few years after that, when crunk was bubbling out of
Atlanta and enjoying a moment as music's hottest trend, Lil Jon
insisted on calling Ciara the Princess of Crunk 'n' B. There is some

representational pride in those nicknames, and they may have helped position those women in ways that mass audiences were ready to understand, but they also imply something "lesser" than sheer pop stardom. It was enough of a challenge for a *pop star* to land a *Vogue* or *Rolling Stone* cover in those days; the Princess of Crunk 'n' B probably didn't stand a chance.

On the flip side, the few Black artists who did get regular approval from industry gatekeepers via awards and legacy media struggled to seem like they were on the cutting edge. Take Keys, a high school valedictorian and child piano prodigy with cover-girl good looks who signed to Clive Davis's J Records in 1998. That was actually her second record deal; her first was with Columbia, where she'd worked briefly with a rotation of outside producers who tried to craft her as an upbeat pop-R&B singer in fitting with the moment. Keys hated the process, and very little of that music got released, but the experience did lead her to spend time writing and producing by herself. By the time she got out of her Columbia deal and signed with J Records, she'd already written what would be her first single and definitive hit, the simple, bluesy, and beautiful "Fallin'."

Davis had been introduced to Keys by Michelle Santosuosso, at the time the VP of crossover music at J Records, a job that often had her working to identify the soul, hip-hop, and R&B records and artists who she felt would resonate with Top 40 audiences. Santosuosso had heard Keys for the first time on the advice of Jermaine Dupri, who had given her a So So Def Christmas sampler album that included Keys's cover of "Little Drummer Boy." Santosuosso felt that Keys was special, and she felt doubly sure that "Fallin'" was special once she heard it, but she also knew it would face challenges in crossing over. "I remember Clive playing 'Fallin'' in our A&R meeting and it was just brilliant," Santosuosso said in our interview.

"But it was also a ballad, and that was really challenging because it was an era of super up-tempo hip-hop music, and that song started extremely slow." Part of Santosuosso's job was to call radio programmers and lobby for the song. "Fallin'" heats up midway through, when a drum loop that sounds an awful lot like a sample of James Brown's "It's A Man's Man's Man's World" kicks in, but it's not a song for the club, which was a problem. "I'm not playing that gospel record," the programmers would tell Santosuosso, who'd end calls shocked by how they were writing off the song. "I'd get so angry, like scream at them and berate them. And Clive would be like, 'Michelle, you cannot scream at the program directors.'"

Santosuosso was right, "Fallin'" *was* a hit. In 2001, the song debuted at number ninety-eight with a slow but steady climb ahead, and despite the challenges of its tempo, a couple of factors were working in its favor. The first was a technological advent not unlike the ones that helped reveal hip-hop's popularity in the early nineties: the adoption of the Arbitron Portable People Meter, which detected what listeners were consuming, for Nielsen testing. The People Meter gave radio stations actual data about the songs their listeners wanted to hear and which ones made them change the dial. It revealed that "Fallin'" was not turning audiences away—quite the opposite. The second factor was Davis's Rolodex. Determined to get a spotlight on Keys, he called in a favor from Oprah, who had Keys come perform "Fallin'" in front of an at-home audience of over ten million on her ratings-leading daytime television show. "After Alicia appeared on *Oprah,* women started calling the radio stations," Santosuosso said. "And that's what helped us break that record."

"Fallin'" hit number one after a ten-week climb. It ended the year as the second-biggest single of 2001. Keys received six Grammy nominations and won five, including Best R&B Album and Song of the Year. For Best New Artist, which was presented by the illustrious duo of Kevin James and Ray Romano, she beat out India.Arie, Nelly Furtado, David Gray, and Linkin Park. *Songs in A Minor,* Keys's debut album, sold seven million copies, making her both a critical darling and someone who moved a ton of inventory. Her second record, *The Diary of Alicia Keys,* sold eight million copies; 2007's *As I Am* sold seven million, and on and on—Alicia Keys has now sold over ninety million albums and won fifteen Grammys.

But while artists like Mary J. Blige, Ashanti, or Ciara were often boxed in by their association with musical trends, Keys came off as such a classicist that she seemed above them altogether. Perhaps this was by design—Keys had outright rejected Columbia's urgings to make up-tempo pop R&B. But she was in conversation with artists like Erykah Badu, the Roots, and Macy Gray, who made up a vibrant neo-soul movement adjacent to pop-R&B artists, and her backbeats often hinted at a fluency with nineties rap. Still, you tended to hear the words "piano prodigy" a lot. In her performance on *Oprah,* she incorporated Beethoven's "Für Elise" into the "Fallin'" intro. It was more common to hear comparisons between Keys and old-school soul divas like Aretha Franklin than it was to hear her discussed as a member of a current musical movement.

Keys also never shared a lot about her personal life or lived in a way that provided chum for the tabloids. She dated her collaborator Kerry "Krucial" Brothers in her early days until they broke up amicably and continued to work together. In 2010, she married Swizz Beatz, with whom she does a lot of humanitarian work and collects a lot of art, which honestly sounds great. Again, she probably wanted it this way—winning a truckload of Grammys and staying out of *Page Six* sounds pretty good from where I'm sitting. It was never Alicia Keys's job to become a true *pop star,* and it almost certainly wasn't her aim—but that is probably the point. On the rare occasion that traditionally white, elite, celebrity spaces did get behind a Black female artist, they tended to present those artists as so *exceptional* as to exclude them from the messier, more tangible celebrity zeitgeist entirely.

I don't know if Beyoncé set out to break through those barriers when she began recording "Crazy in Love." That's a lot of pressure to put on a song. Then again, *history in the making,* the man said. But even without that weight, "Crazy in Love" had fairly high stakes as far as singles go, since it was the first release from her debut solo album, 2003's *Dangerously in Love,* which marked her departure from Destiny's Child. The girl group had gone on hiatus after 2001's *Survivor* so all the members could pursue solo music, and Beyoncé Knowles's was the most highly anticipated. Beyoncé had always been the It Girl of Destiny's Child, the one everyone assumed had the best chance to make it as a solo star. This anointing was the subject of some controversy—mostly because her father, Mathew Knowles, was also Destiny's Child's manager—though it seems safe to say it has stood the test of time. So *Dangerously in Love* carried the brunt of all those expectations, and its first single was the first chance to meet them. You can understand, then, why for her solo arrival she wanted a full thirty seconds of intro to make sure everyone was properly seated.

While she was recording the album, Beyoncé also took on the role of Foxxy Cleopatra in the third *Austin Powers* movie (yes) and recorded an original song for the soundtrack, "Work It Out." If this sounds like a really cheesy thing for Beyoncé to have done, let me remind you that in 2001, Destiny's Child performed as part of George W. Bush's inauguration, and Beyoncé tried to get a "Let me hear you say Buuuuuuuuuuuush!" chant going in the crowd—she had some stumbles on her way to being the deft image crafter she is today. "Work It Out" is funky, and Beyoncé sells it, but it never even broke onto the Hot 100. On a perhaps related note, the music video is a supercut of Beyoncé singing in a gold minidress with Mike Myers in character making crazy faces. We have all made mistakes.

Around the same time "Work It Out" flopped, fellow Destiny's Child alum Kelly Rowland did the best thing one could do in the summer of 2002, which was get on a Nelly track. Kelly sang the hook of "Dilemma," which followed "Hot in Herre" to the top of the charts as part of a seventeen-week reign at number one. Kelly had a hit and Beyoncé didn't and since they were both Columbia Records artists, the label didn't want them stepping on each other's toes. (Michelle Williams also had a number-one gospel album at the time, which was not as big a deal but part of this calculus, too.) Columbia decided to ride the hot hand, rushing Kelly's album out and delaying Beyoncé's, which gave her some extra time to work on it. With that time, she recorded "Crazy in Love."

The story of the making of the song goes like this: Beyoncé reached out to new producers, including Rich Harrison, who'd worked with Mary J. Blige and the R&B artist Amerie. Harrison had this riff he was excited about, one he'd been saving for the right moment, built around the Chi-Lites' doo-wop groove and those psychedelic horns. When Beyoncé called, Harrison had his moment. He'd been sitting on that beat. He felt in his bones the track was the beat to a hit record. In 2004, he told MTV he was initially surprised that Beyoncé didn't immediately agree with him when he played it for her. It wasn't that she didn't like it, she just felt it was unfinished. "I love the idea," she told him. "Now write the song, I'll be back in two hours."

Beyoncé was heading out to buy Kelly Rowland a birthday present, but she was not loving her outfit. She kept looking in the mirror, checking her hair and her clothes, and repeating one phrase: "I look *crazy* right now." That was Harrison's a-ha moment: That was the hook. By the time Beyoncé returned, he'd written the chorus and the verses. That was enough for her to agree that this was a song they should record, and she added the bridge and all the "uh-ohs." But the song still needed one more element.

At the time she was recording *Dangerously in Love,* Beyoncé was publicly cagey about whether she was dating the rapper Jay-Z. They were out and about together a lot, but they wouldn't say what was up. They'd met in 2000, when they shared a plane ride to Cancún to film performances for MTV's Spring Break, natch. But Jay was notoriously hard to pin down; he'd cultivated an image as the ultimate bachelor. He was never in a serious relationship. When he sang on the Mariah Carey song "Heartbreaker," the whole point of the feature was that *he* was the heartbreaker. He loved to rap about being a player. How he'd never give his heart to a woman. Here's a couple more lines of Jay on his relationship status:

Got a condo with nothin' but condoms in it

Also:

All I do is rap and sex

So, yeah, Jay was a bit of a fuckboy! He was the undisputed king of New York rap, what did you expect? He had asked Beyoncé to join him on "'03 Bonnie & Clyde," which, at the suggestion of then producer Kanye West, used a sample from Tupac's "Me and My Girlfriend." It was a clever commentary on the maybe-relationship that allowed Bey and Jay to play into the rumors without actually confirming anything (and for Jay to rap the line: *Only time we don't speak is during* Sex and the City). But "'03 Bonnie & Clyde" was on Jay's album and ultimately on Jay's terms.

"Crazy in Love" was by, for, and about Beyoncé. Sure, in his verse, Jay mostly raps about how great he is. Beyoncé, narratively, is the one who is bugging out in love. But there's no confusing who the star of "Crazy in Love" is, and who the catch of "Crazy in Love" is—only one person on the song is introduced with literal fanfare. The night before the album was due, Beyoncé called Jay-Z up and asked him to come in and rap on the song, and he drove right to the studio just to go hype her up. I think in the "Crazy in Love" intro you can hear the moment Jay realizes he wants to spend a lifetime building an empire and occasionally crashing Carroll Gardens pizzerias with Beyoncé. That is a hell of a way to hard launch your relationship—and your solo career.

"Crazy in Love" hit number one and stayed there for eight consecutive weeks. It was the only single released ahead of *Dangerously in Love*, which debuted atop the *Billboard* 200 albums chart. Beyoncé already had a sizable fan base coming out of Destiny's Child—getting "bootylicious" added to the dictionary counts for a lot—but very quickly, she was one of the most famous women in the world. Between 2003 and 2004, she covered *Harper's Bazaar, Rolling Stone, Glamour, InStyle, Vanity Fair, Elle,* and *Cosmopolitan.* She became a popular Halloween costume—the opening frames of the Jake Nava–directed "Crazy in Love" music video, in which Beyoncé struts down a street in denim hot pants, a white (Prada) tank, and red Stuart Weitzmans, had been designed to be imitable. She became a regular fixture of Met Galas and Oscars—for the 2005 Academy Awards, at which she performed a record *three* times, she wore black Versace and a reported *fifty-two pounds* of diamonds. That is as A-list as it gets.

All the while, as her celebrity grew, Beyoncé remained in touch with the center of pop music. *Dangerously in Love* had another number one on its track list, the Sean Paul collab "Baby Boy," plus the Donna Summer interpolating "Naughty Girl," which went to number three. (Acclaim was not universal—*The New York Times* review ran under the retroactively hilarious headline: "The Solo Beyoncé: She's No Ashanti.") Destiny's Child had promised to get back together for a fourth and final album, 2004's *Destiny Fulfilled*, which delayed the release of Beyoncé's sophomore album *B'Day* until 2006, but it arrived stacked with surprising, funk-filled hits like "Freakum Dress" and "Ring the Alarm," with many more to follow. She has had ebbs and flows of sheer chart dominance, but as of this writing, in her third decade of work, Beyoncé remains a hitmaker, a dedicated archivist of historically Black popular music, and a near-deified figure in the celebrity world. By now it feels inadequate to simply call Beyoncé a pop star, but in the first chapters of her solo career, that title represented the elusive space she'd won: Beyoncé was both a true, A-list pop star, and a good representative of the music that was defining the pop landscape.

A weird but fascinating thing to acknowledge is how essential Jay-Z was to pulling all that off. A significant portion of the heat around Beyoncé's early solo work came from playing into the mystery around their relationship, then displaying herself proudly as the woman who'd locked down a notorious bachelor. It's a somewhat confounding dynamic from someone who'd go on to be one of pop's most prominent feminists—one who gained some attention in 2024 when Jay-Z was accused in a lawsuit of raping a teenage girl at a party in 2003 alongside Sean "Diddy" Combs, allegations he has denied—but it's also a contradiction that's been a lasting throughline of Mrs. Carter's career. In 2008, a half decade after "Crazy in Love," Beyoncé used the music video for her award-winning and independence-celebrating hit "Single Ladies," to debut her twenty-four-carat diamond engagement ring.

Jay often seemed to cosign Beyoncé's raciest moments. On the podcast *Making Beyoncé,* from NPR's Chicago station WBEZ, Knowles's marketing director, Quincy Jackson, described embracing sexuality—letting the world see Beyoncé as a woman, not a member of a girl group—as a major shift around her solo career. Destiny's Child always sang about relationships through the lens of their power dynamics and their internal politics, but they were rarely if ever raunchy—Destiny's Child is at the club at *11:30.* If I have to be at the club, that is when I want to be at the club, but you and I both know that isn't when things are really happening at the club. And as a solo artist, when Beyoncé turned things up a notch, she often did so through the lens of her relationship with Jay.

This is not to say that she made herself his sex object. Jay-Z is in the "Crazy in Love" music video, but he does almost nothing other than set a car on fire for no discernible reason and stand still so Beyoncé can dance around him. She manages to do this in a way that's all about *her.* Beyoncé does plenty of dancing around Jay-Z in the "'03 Bonnie & Clyde" video, which tells an on-the-run story in which the two of them drive across the border and evade police, who are played by the cast of *The Wire.* But there, she's always looking at Jay because she's dancing *for* him. In the "Crazy in Love" video, there's a ton of eye contact with the camera, but basically none with Jay. He's not there when Beyoncé kicks open a fire hydrant to soak herself as the camera pans over her body or when she dances in front of a massive fan in a plunging off-the-runway Versace minidress. Still, these moments of liberated spectacle come paired with Beyoncé's celebration of herself as one half of a power couple.

Perhaps this was a calculated move. Perhaps Beyoncé knew leaning into her relationship would give her more freedom to make wilder, more lustful music within the safety of monogamous bliss. Perhaps she was just super hot for Jay! I know we've all now seen those photos of him riding a Jet Ski in a helmet, but he was a real Romeo at the time. Maybe she just knew that celebrity relationships are a great way for the public to get invested in everyone's business—in any case, it certainly wound up working that way.

By the time she was making *B'Day,* Bey and Jay were very public, having made their red carpet debut together at the 2005 Oscars. There were also a whole bunch of rumors swirling around blogs and tabloids that Jay-Z was cheating, potentially with Rihanna, who he'd signed to Def Jam Records the year before. It was quite easy to read that subtext into *B'Day. Lemonade* included, there is still no more quintessentially Beyoncé take on infidelity than "Ring the Alarm," in which she channels the fury of finding out her man is a cheat through the funk-filled club stomping nightmare of imagining his other woman inhabiting her luxe life with him—rocking her chinchilla coats and her VVS stones, driving her Rolls to their house on the coast. It is one of the best songs in her discography, and, in hindsight especially, the relationship perspective it shows of partnership as love and support, but also as shared wealth and power, makes it one of her most authentic, contradictions and all. Still, the song off *B'Day* that got the most attention as a "Jay cheated" anthem was the ballad "Irreplaceable," which went to number one and birthed one thousand memes of *to the left, to the left.*

The irony of this is that in reality, there is no way that "Irreplaceable" was actually about Jay. Ne-Yo was the actual songwriter, and the idea that all of Jay-Z's earthly possessions fit in one single box, which in the music video contained two books and a single basketball trophy, is absurd. *This man said he has a condo full of nothing but condoms.* But that's the mark of a true pop star: When it's impossible to tell where the songs end and the persona begins, it's there.

Beyoncé had basically one more album left in what I'd call her pure–pop star phase. In 2008, she released *I Am . . . Sasha Fierce,* a concept record with dueling sides representing the split personalities of her real-life and stage personas—the Sasha Fierce side represented by bops like "Single Ladies" or "Diva," and the I Am . . . side by ballads like "Halo" and "If I Were a Boy." It's not my favorite Beyoncé album, but it does stand as a button on her first era when she was primarily evaluated in the terms of mainstream pop success. Barack Obama was elected president two weeks before *I Am . . . Sasha Fierce* was released, and Beyoncé performed Etta James's "At Last" for the first couple at the inauguration ceremony in 2009. It was a choice full of symbolism, both for the song's audience and for its performer. At the time of its release in 1961, "At Last" struggled on pop radio—it never got above number forty-seven—because it was considered "too Black" for those audiences. It was around the time of this performance that Beyoncé seemed to graduate from "mere" pop stardom. She was not done making hits or headlines, but she had so much that simply chasing more seemed to trivialize her intent. Yet as she ascended, she left a new picture of pop stardom in her own image.

Beyoncé took three years off between *I Am . . . Sasha Fierce* and her fourth album, *4.* During that time, she let her father go as her manager. She made it clear her focus was on auteurship, not chart dominance. In 2013, she dropped an entire visual album one night in December without any warning. She became far less accessible to the press; in 2015, she covered *Vogue*'s September issue without participating in a feature story, which had not happened in that magazine in at least five years. She stopped tweeting—Beyoncé today does one single weird online thing: She posts celebrity baby photos on her website to wish them happy birthday. Most importantly, she began to write the stories of the Black diaspora more explicitly into her albums.

These were impactful, often thrilling shifts. And I would like to put it on the record that I have felt no small amount of trepidation toward opining at length on ~the meaning of Beyoncé.~ But while I think Beyoncé has honed her craft since the mid-2000s—she has certainly gotten better at inaugural performances—I do think the idea of a true before and after shortchanges what she accomplished in her first decade and the most radical moments on her first three solo albums. There's a great *SNL* sketch from 2016, not long after Beyoncé released *Lemonade,* the album in which she wrote the story of Jay-Z's infidelities into the history of Black women's mistreatment, marginalization, solidarity, and strength. The sketch is a fake trailer for a movie called *The Day Beyoncé Turned Black.* In it, a bunch of white people hear the song "Formation" for the first time, and completely lose their minds at one of their favorite pop stars using music and words they don't understand. *"Hot sauce in my bag, swag? What does that even mean,"* wonders a distraught Beck Bennett. *"I don't think this song is for us,"* worries Bobby Moynihan. *"BUT USUALLY EVERYTHING IS!!!"* shrieks Cecily Strong. By the end of the trailer, cut in the mode of a horror movie, Kate McKinnon suffocates her small child with a pillow, saving him from a world that has been transformed in terrifying ways. As she pushes the cushion down over him, she sings the hook from "Single Ladies." *Uh-oh uh-ohhhh. . . .*

Extremely good bit. Go back and watch it, it'll be a good palate cleanser before I overanalyze four minutes of sketch comedy. Are you done? Cool. Because I have to ask—would the last beat have worked with "Ring the Alarm," "Get Me Bodied," or the herky-jerky confidence of "Freakum Dress"? The sounds of those songs were fresh, complex, even strange to a mainstream pop audience in the mid-aughts, but because Beyoncé made them hits, listeners gained a broader understanding of what a pop song can be or sound like, and who can sing one. In a decade in which hip-hop and R&B became the underlying sounds of modern popular music, Beyoncé broke down barriers that kept artists from those worlds, especially Black women, from reaching the highest echelons of pop stardom. Without her, would pop-fluent rappers like Nicki Minaj, or even Drake, seem so self-evidently part of the culture of both mainstream music and elite celebrity? Would Top 40 audiences be regularly exposed to thesis-driven projects about the history of Black art forms in the United States like *Renaissance* and *Cowboy Carter*? As Beyoncé remains one of the biggest pop stars working, it's impossible to define the world she has left in her wake. But ever since she broke into that rarefied group around her solo debut, the world of pop stardom has been in closer step with the charts and with pop music because of her. History in the making, indeed.

6

Kelly Clarkson, Manic Pixie Dream Girl

IN 2004, ALTERNATIVE ROCK FOUND ITSELF IN SOME UN-expected places, including Natalie Portman's headphones. "You've got to hear this song," said Portman, in character to Zach Braff, in the movie *Garden State*, which premiered on July 28 of that year. "It'll change your life." She handed over the set and her Walkman, out of which came the gentle harmonies of the Shins' "New Slang." The darling of the 2004 Sundance Film Festival and a surprising hit in its time, *Garden State* has come to stand for some of the decade's well-worn indie clichés, including its hipstercore soundtrack and, especially, its deployment through Portman's character Sam of a particular trope that would become known as the manic pixie dream girl. That actual phrase was coined in 2007, when the critic Nathan Rabin described a ubiquitous character type who "exists solely in the fevered imaginations of sensitive writer-directors to teach broodingly soulful young men to embrace life and its infinite mysteries and adventures," in his review of *Elizabethtown* for *The*

A.V. Club. The MPDG at the center of that review was Kirsten Dunst's Claire Colburn, but she and Natalie were not alone. MPDGs could be blond or brunette, Kate Winslet in wigs (*Eternal Sunshine of the Spotless Mind*) or on a boat with Ben Stiller (Jennifer Aniston in *Along Came Polly*), but the defining feature they shared—the source of much eventual derision of this trope—was that they were whatever the male characters they played opposite needed and wanted them to be. And with comic frequency, what that involved was being doting fans of the NPR-core hipster-pop that was dominating the indie music scene.

In *Elizabethtown,* Dunst gives Orlando Bloom mixtapes of Cameron Crowe's favorite songs, a jumble of Ryan Adams, Tom Petty, and, yes, the Shins. In *The Perks of Being a Wallflower,* Emma Watson's Sam thinks records sound better on vinyl. On the Fox teen soap *The O.C.,* Adam Brody's Seth Cohen spends a fair bit of time processing romantic partners based on their appreciation of Death Cab for Cutie—though he does end up with Summer, who deems it "one guitar and a whole lot of complaining." *Almost Famous*'s Penny Lane is both a groupie and a muse to the fictional up-and-coming rock band Stillwater. And then there's Natalie Portman's Sam, who thinks the Shins can change your life.

Of course, the Manic Pixie Dream Girl trope revealed something about the era's relationship to women, but it also revealed something about its relationship to indie, which really revealed something about its relationship to *taste.* The Manic Pixie Dream Girl is the saving grace of any disenchanted male protagonist because she's *not like other girls,* which is, of course, why she likes indie rock, presumably as opposed to pop. The quirkiness was the point.

It was around the time of these movies, in the mid-aughts, that I remember catching on to the idea that liking things was not merely for enjoyment's sake but for what the things you liked said about who you were. This revelation was mostly a product of my age, but as social media and internet blogs proliferated in the early 2000s, tastemaking in general was also taking on a newish role in culture writ large. Affinity was once a more practical matter; it told you which bins to sift through in a record store or what magazine to subscribe to to learn about new releases or what club to show up at. The internet, though, made pretty much any music accessible within a few clicks. Gaining access to music in the first place was no longer a great expression of fandom, but *choosing* something within the quickly expanding array of options available to everyone was meaningful, especially if it was something most others weren't choosing. It was during this time I had my first "boyfriend," a floppy-haired boy who took me to a dance and who I made out with a few times. We hung out for about a month, much of which was spent talking about indie rock bands I sort of liked, but was mostly pretending to think were mind-blowingly amazing, and I probably over-internalized a few comments about how songs I brought up were *so mainstream.* This was the era of *I liked them before they were cool* as an earnest brag, one that carried the same implication as most manic pixie dream girl playlists: that there were indie records, and they were *much* cooler than mine.

The twist of this dynamic was that it took the niche and made it cool, which then made it *popular.* Some of the most taste-making soundtracks of this era were on teen soaps like *The O.C.* and, later, *Gossip Girl,* which got millions of young people—myself included!—into Peter Bjorn and John, Phoenix, and Muse. (It's funny to think back and remember how a lot of the same songs I used to endear myself to guys in class by letting them think they'd shown me them for the first time were actually tracks I'd heard while Dan and Serena were making out.) And for all the indie signaling of a movie like *Garden State,* Fox Searchlight bought it out of Sundance in a bidding war and promoted the living daylights out of it. And for all the retrospective teasing of its dated tropes, when these movies were actually coming out, basics like me went positively feral for their wistful tales of coastal white boy ennui. The worst-kept secret of mid-aughts hipsterdom was that it was painfully mainstream.

A lasting change the aughts brought to our pop-cultural landscape was the erosion of the boundaries between pop and indie, hitmaker and tastemaker. As mounting financial pressures coaxed indie bands into mass-marketed spaces like network television, popular romantic comedies, and even advertising, many of those bands became genuinely popular, shifting norms around consumerism in traditionally alternative spaces and injecting their musical textures into traditionally popular formats. The immediate impact of this cross-pollination was a wave of rock-inflected pop music that crested between 2005 and 2008, but in the longer term, what mattered most is that the space between the bespoke and the commercial was permanently shrunk. You can tell the story of this collision between pop and indie through the soundtracks of mid-aughts TV and movies, but on the *Billboard* charts themselves, the protagonist is one Kelly Brianne Clarkson, who in the same summer of 2004—just as Natalie was handing over her Walkman and her headphones—changed the future of pop with the song "Since U Been Gone."

If the story of "Since U Been Gone" involves both the marginal and the centrist, Max Martin represents the latter. In early 2004, though, he found himself in a position he wasn't used to: He was old news, in pressing danger of going the way of the Tamagotchi. A *Time* magazine cover had anointed him "The Music Man" in 2001, but he hadn't had a big hit since. The center of pop had reasserted itself around hip-hop producers and R&B hooks, and Britney

Spears was recording songs originally written for Janet Jackson. Martin didn't just need another hit, he needed a new sound: The bright chords and clean new jack swing rhythms were done, and they'd been replaced by funky chromatic chord progressions and off-kilter drum patterns. To simply copy this would have been pointless. Max Martin songs are fundamentally about satisfaction—he gives you what your ear wants to hear—but the sounds of the day were about curiosity, never really knowing what you're hearing or what's coming next. A good example is the chorus in "I'm a Slave 4 U," Spears's first track with the Neptunes. It gets almost no harmonic context from its sparse synthesizer chords—a root chord and another just a semi-tone above—a very *not* Martin approach. And besides, Max Martin is the man who thought ". . . Baby One More Time" should go to TLC. This was just not his wheelhouse. Instead, he spent most of 2002 and 2003 producing for Celine Dion and Michael Bolton.

That was around the time he became friends with Lukasz Gottwald, a.k.a. Dr. Luke—the *Saturday Night Live* house-guitarist-turned-producer who'd go on to work with Avril Lavigne on her late-career pop turn. On one visit to New York, Martin wanted to get some work done and called Gottwald to ask if he could rent his studio. Gottwald, who'd wanted to work with Martin but had been trying to play it cool, told him he should just use it, which endeared Martin. They spent time in that studio together, and at one point, they turned on "Maps," the strange and aching breakout song by the New York–based indie rock band Yeah Yeah Yeahs. The emotional urgency of Karen O's goodbye lament, and her real tears in the music video, won circulation around the internet, traction on digital download charts, and, eventually, a spot on the lower reaches of the Hot 100.

In an earlier era, the Hot 100 wouldn't have been part of the conversation about a band like the Yeah Yeah Yeahs. But indie became centrist in part because its more radical edges got squeezed out, particularly on the radio. In 1996, Congress passed the Telecommunications Act, sweeping media legislation that significantly deregulated broadcasting. Before the law passed, a single radio corporation could own no more than forty stations, with no more than two in a single market. The law increased the market cap to eight and removed the national cap altogether, and by 2001 Clear Channel (now iHeartMedia) had grown from forty stations nationwide to 1,240, with homogenized playlists that played the same songs in heavy rotation. Local rock stations were gobbled up in the machine. Beyond radio, Napster was three years old, and the money-making model behind the industry had been completely upended in a way that could make capitalists out of the most hardened indie snobs. So they did what they could to get heard and, especially, to get paid: Vampire Weekend did Tommy Hilfiger ads; Beck premiered an entire five songs during an episode of *The O.C.* in which Seth, Summer, Ryan, and Marissa get stuck at the mall. A silver lining at the time was that while radio was a harsher gatekeeper than ever, some of the new marketplaces allowed fans to bypass that format. Soundtracks were one avenue. The iTunes Store, also, went online on April 28, 2003, and its download charts would occasionally help a left-of-center hit or two bubble up in this way, which is what happened with "Maps."

As the story goes, as they listened, Dr. Luke commented on how much he liked the song. "Maps" is a classic breakup song—Karen O wants her man to stay—but it's also weird as hell. The word "maps" isn't discernible in the lyrics, she sings it as a long melisma across two full bars of music. Phrases like *wait, they don't love you like I love you*—which if you don't know from Yeah Yeah Yeahs, you may know from Beyoncé's interpolation on "Hold Up" off *Lemonade*—and *oh say say say* are repeated over and over. There are only twenty-six words in the entire song. But there's an addictive quality to the guitar sounds and the verse melody and the breakdown—which on "Maps" is the emotional peak of the entire record. That's what Luke was responding to, and Martin agreed with him—mostly.

A central part of the Max Martin lore is that he's a pretty humble guy. This is usually attributed as a Swedish thing. There's a Scandinavian cultural principle called Jantelagen that discourages anyone from drawing individual attention to themselves. This happens to be a pretty good characteristic for a pop music producer, someone who, by trade, needs to fill a major behind-the-scenes role without taking up any of an artist's limelight. Martin definitely fits this bill—his reputation is as a lighthearted guy who gets along with most people, who avoids self-aggrandizement and turns down almost every interview request that comes his way. But being humble is not the same as lacking confidence, and Max Martin does not hold his opinions loosely.

Rather, his particular musical dogmas can lend themselves to *very* blunt critiques, for better or for worse. In 2014, Martin made Ariana Grande sing nonsense so that "Break Free" would adhere to his principles of melodic math. In 2017, when Lorde consulted him before the release of her sophomore album *Melodrama,* he told her that the song "Green Light" was "incorrect" songwriting and "a strange piece of music." Lorde brought that up in a *New York Times Magazine* profile and also said that Martin didn't mean it as an insult, that's just how he is. I think you have to understand this about Martin to understand his response to Luke on "Maps," a popular and critically celebrated song of raw emotion that's also genuinely avant-garde, which was as follows: "If they would just write a damn pop chorus on it!" If indie was already inching toward the mainstream before the fall of 2004, the moment Martin lamented to Dr. Luke, with a straight face, that the iconoclastic Karen O hadn't paid enough attention to the *don't bore us, get to the chorus!* school of hitmaking was when whatever space was left between pop and indie collapsed for good.

After that conversation, Martin and Dr. Luke decided to give a go of *writing a damn pop chorus* on top of "Maps" themselves. They took the breakdown of the song—the drawn out "maps" and the "they don't love you like I love yous"—and spun the instrumentals into the skeleton of a chorus, one that sounded less like something you'd hear from an act at a club on the Bowery and more like something from one of the eighties arena rock bands Martin was so fond of. They kept it as a breakup song, but fitting with its glossy musical makeover, reshaped the message to be about the relief of being done with an ex who'd left, of finally getting what you want, of being *so moving on.* They called it "Since U Been Gone."

Because of that bombastic chorus, Martin and Dr. Luke needed to find a vocalist with metric tons of lung capacity to record the song. But they also wanted someone cool. Recall that Martin had fallen off the cutting edge, so he wanted the right kind of street cred to fuel his comeback. He initially imagined the song for Pink, but she turned it down. It was then offered to Hilary Duff, but she didn't have the range for it. As Martin and Dr. Luke shopped the track around, Clive Davis, the head of RCA Records, got wind of it and suggested it go to Kelly Clarkson, the young Texan with a big voice who'd won the first season of *American Idol* with the heartfelt ballad "A Moment Like This," and earned a contract with his label. Initially, Martin was not into the idea. He may not have been fully aware of the power of Clarkson's voice, a three-octave power tool with the capacity to belt far into its upper reaches. He may also have been *too* aware that he found *American Idol* to be a little tacky.

"They weren't prepared for the casting idea," Davis told *Billboard* in 2010. "Max was looking to move on from what he had done with Backstreet Boys, and I really spent time convincing them that an *American Idol* winner could bring all the feeling and passion that was required to the song." Davis did his cajoling, and when Clarkson jumped up an octave on the chorus while recording her demo, that did the rest.

I'm not sure Max Martin knew quite what he had in "Since U Been Gone," at least not at first. That's partly due to his skepticism over Clarkson, but it's mostly about the other artists he thought made sense for the song. Pink could have worked—she'd have played up the edge and the rasp. But suggesting "Since U Been Gone" for Hilary Duff makes me think Martin thought of it as a good breakup song with hooks, instead of an emo-pop rager. Kelly Clarkson was destined to sing "Since U Been Gone," and there's no one on earth who could have done a better job with that song (but if it hadn't gone to her it should have gone to a band like Fall Out Boy). "Since U Been Gone" is a song for an artist with a preposterously huge voice—and that's Kelly Clarkson.

In pop, the song was responsible for some tectonic shifts. It's hard to pin down the combination of guitar textures, arena-rock bombast, Clarkson's jet propulsion vocals, and the glossy weightlessness of Martin and Dr. Luke's production by genre alone, but the combination definitely didn't add up to the crunk and R&B that made up most of Top 40 in 2003 and 2004. Maybe that's the underground spirit of "Maps" bubbling up through the song, though the end result of "Since U Been Gone" sounds almost nothing like "Maps," either. "Maps" is all fuzz, static, and eccentricity, while "Since U Been Gone" operates with blunt force. In any case, it worked—"Since U Been Gone" quickly became a massive hit. It would have gone to number one on the Hot 100 were it not for the eternal power of 50 Cent's "Candy Shop," but the song reached number two and stayed on the chart for a whopping forty-six weeks. At its peak, it was the highest-charting song by a female solo artist outside of R&B that year. Not everyone loved it—Karen O called it "poisonous varmint," but that's Karen O, who like Max Martin, has her own particular dogmas.

One lasting impact of "Since U Been Gone" is that it proved Max Martin still had the magic touch. It was also the song that made Dr. Luke an in-demand producer. After "Since U Been Gone," the pair became the force behind a wave of rock-oriented pop that tried to build on its success. Together, they produced songs like "Feels Like Tonight" for Daughtry, "4ever" and "Everything I'm Not" for the Veronicas, "Girlfriend" for Avril Lavigne, and "U + Ur Hand" for Pink—chatspeak had worked its way particularly well into semi-bratty pop-rock song titles. This work gave Martin a second act, which would prove to not be his last, but was critical to his ascension as the defining hitmaker of the twenty-first century because it showed his skills transcended teen pop. Meanwhile it became Dr. Luke's on-ramp to becoming a prolific hitmaker in the late aughts and through the 2010s. Dr. Luke has a complicated legacy—his impact on pop in that era is indelible, but he's been accused of horrible abuses by Kesha, the artist for whom he produced defining hits, and described as, at minimum, a really shitty dude by many other women in music.

Another impact of "Since U Been Gone" was that it was the hit that made Kelly Clarkson a huge star outside of *Idol* (and proved that *Idol* was capable of finding someone with that capacity). Not everything about this was good from Clarkson's point of view, because succeeding on that plane put the pressure on for more hits. For Max Martin and Dr. Luke, getting the hit was the point. For Kelly Clarkson, the value of "Since U Been Gone" was more nuanced. Clarkson badly wanted to jump-start her career as a recording artist—before she tried out for *American Idol*, she'd turned down multiple music conservatory scholarship offers, moved to Los Angeles, and waited tables, because she felt she could get a big break faster on her own. But she wasn't purely interested in hitmaking. Music was a key way Clarkson processed the trauma of her childhood, particularly her relationship with her alcoholic father who'd left her mother when Kelly was six, taking her older brother with him, sending her sister to live with an aunt, and leaving Kelly at home with her mother. The songs she wrote herself tended to be dark and emotional along the lines of the ballad "Because of You," which she wrote for *Breakaway* with Ben Moody and David Hodges from Evanescence. And to Clarkson, pop success was more valuable as a means to making a good living recording the music that meant the most to her than it was for its own sake alone.

But once she'd had a major hit like "Since U Been Gone," along with additional singles "Breakaway," "Behind These Hazel Eyes," and "Because of You"—which she fought hard to have on the album—and *Breakaway* went on to multiplatinum success, the pressure was on to keep producing smashes, particularly from Davis. For the twelve years and six album cycles between the release of *Breakaway* and when Clarkson's contract with Davis's RCA expired in 2016, the two were regularly at odds over creative control—Kelly demanding the freedom to record the music she wanted to make and Davis demanding more "Since U Been Gone" varietals. Clarkson had not even liked recording "Since U Been Gone" in the first place—Davis wrote in his 2013 memoir that she hadn't wanted to sing the song or let it go on the record, a claim that Bravo's Andy Cohen brought up to Clarkson in a 2023 appearance on *Watch What Happens Live*. "Let's give some backstory," Clarkson replied. "I was lied to." Clarkson said she was told that she'd be involved in writing the song and that the producers had been working with dummy lyrics. Her label flew her to Sweden to record with Max and Luke, and Clarkson felt embarrassed when she got there expecting to be a bigger part of the process and found that the song was done. She was just there to sing. Her hurt feelings about the pretense were among the first major issues between Clarkson and Clive Davis. They were far from the last.

In his memoir, Davis also wrote about how often Clarkson would break down in tears in his office. In a response on her website after the memoir came out, Clarkson said that she had indeed cried in front of the mogul after playing him "Because of You," which, according to Clarkson's post, Davis did not like. "I cried because he hated it and told me verbatim that I was 'a shitty writer who should be grateful for the gifts that he bestows upon me,'" she wrote. That blog post has long since been deleted, but it's memorialized in John Seabrook's excellent book *The Song Machine*, which contains a whole chapter called "The Ballad of Kelly and Clive." There is a lot of back and forth, but it boils down to this: Clarkson wanted to make the songs she wanted to make, Davis wanted her to make hits, and he probably wasn't the most tactful about expressing this. After the success of *Breakaway*, Clarkson felt like she'd earned some creative freedom, and fought intensely with Davis to let her record the confessional record she'd always wanted to make. She cowrote every song on 2007's *My December* and resisted significant pressure to make the album less angry, or to work with big-name producers. Davis was pretty livid about this, but he acquiesced. The only problem was that the album flopped, and it probably flopped mostly because there is no "Since U Been Gone" on *My December*. RCA could have been a lot more helpful in the promotion of the record, but the album sold about a tenth of what *Breakaway* did, and Clarkson fired her manager and canceled her tour. I'm team Kelly, but I also think if you can have a song like "Since U Been Gone" on your album, you should probably do that.

The story of "Since U Been Gone" shows the increasingly broad intersection of pop and indie in the mid-aughts, but it also shows the lasting friction between those identities. In the same way that bands like the Killers were making the defining music of teen soaps, a song like "Maps" could trickle up into the highest echelons of major-label hitmaking. At the same time, when a pop artist like Clarkson wanted to pursue making music that didn't chase the *Billboard* charts, she faced a lot of pushback. In the aftermath, though, the barriers dissolved further. Though her label was pushing pop stardom for its own sake, "Since U Been Gone" did win Clarkson a kind of status as your favorite rocker's favorite pop star. The indie rocker Ted Leo started covering the song at shows. Clarkson had a brief dalliance with Yellowcard front man Ryan Key, at one point during which the two drunkenly got onstage and sang during a night out after seeing the hair metal cover band Steel Panther.

In the following years, more alt sounds bubbled up into the pop mainstream. In 2008, the Clash-sampling song "Paper Planes," by the antagonistic electro/hip-hop artist M.I.A., surprisingly became a mainstream hit. By the early 2010s, alternative groups like fun., Neon Trees, Gotye, and M83 had a meaningful place on Top 40 radio. Beyoncé was going to Grizzly Bear shows in Williamsburg. Alternative was able to be a little bit more pop, and pop itself developed a middle class of stars that were pop in the aesthetic and musical senses but could have the type of niche success more typical of alternative music. A year after *Breakaway*, Swedish pop artist Robyn, who less than a decade earlier had been the blueprint for Britney Spears, released her eponymous fourth album, an arena-filling dance record that was also teeming with indie strangeness. It was bigger as a pure hit in the United Kingdom than the United

States, but *Robyn* was lauded by critics and established Robyn herself as credible both as a hitmaker and an indie weirdo. The longer she thrived in both spaces the less the distinction seemed necessary.

At the beginning of the 2000s, indie and pop were separate, delineated spaces. They were different aesthetically, sure, but also separated into distinct financial structures. Cross-pollination was rare, even scandalous. By the end of the decade, though, those borders had dissolved. In the mid-aughts, indie artists started working their way into the mainstream through commercials and network TV soundtracks. And starting with Kelly Clarkson and "Since U Been Gone," the pop hitmaking machine itself brought indie into its mainstream. Those textures remained—in 2016, Vampire Weekend front-man-turned-producer Ezra Koenig interpolated "Maps," the same song that inspired "Since U Been Gone," into a track "Hold Up," for Beyoncé. Having indie luminaries like Koenig demonstrate an interest in pop music helped transfer some indie credibility onto pop stars. It's harder to scoff that music is *so mainstream* when key figures from the fringes are endorsing it, and harder still when the barriers between the mainstream and those fringes dissolve altogether. The relationship that developed between pop and indie in the 2000s has led to some excellent music, and it has taught audiences that it's possible for pop music to include depth and eccentricity, even within massive hits like "Since U Been Gone."

And for pop stars themselves, that flexibility has made it easier for artists in the wake of these changes to explore more and less commercial music. Clarkson struggled with her label immediately after "Since U Been Gone" because she wanted to record songs that meant something to her beyond just making hits, but the label impulse at the time was to tell her that making hits is what pop stars do. But by pushing back, and as part of this shift that connected indie spaces with pop spaces, Clarkson made it possible for an artist like Charli XCX to chart a career in the years that came after that was equal parts hitmaking and avant-garde. Clarkson was at the center of the collision of pop and indie in the 2000s, which undercut the idea that the indie records were so much cooler after all.

7

Miss Bad Media Karma

IN THE WEE HOURS OF NOVEMBER 29, 2006, BRITNEY Spears, Paris Hilton, and Lindsay Lohan exited the club at the Beverly Hilton in Los Angeles. Looking reckless and carefree, they piled into the front seat of Hilton's Mercedes-Benz SLR McLaren. Camera clicks from a hoard of onlooking paparazzi rang through the air like cicadas, flashbulbs reflected off fresh coats of pale pink lip gloss as the women were photographed through the windshield. "Oh this is classic," said one pap, sounding thirsty. This was no ordinary club scene. The bimbos, they were summiting.

That phrase—"Bimbo Summit"—was what the *New York Post* infamously plastered across its front page in that day's edition, which included a full accounting of the observed behavior of the unholy trinity of naughty aughties tabloid coverage. (The *Post*, at this time, was *obsessed* with using the word "bimbo." They called 2007 the "Year of the Bimbo." Anyone in low-rise Juicy Couture within eyesight of a *Page Six* photographer was in danger.) The assumed agenda of said summit was a little like Vienna, 1961, by way of Sunset Boulevard: acknowledging the cooling of an ongoing drama between Lohan and Hilton over Greek shipping heir Stavros Niarchos III. Niarchos was an on-again, off-again boyfriend of Hilton's who Lohan had been spotted out with during one of the "off" periods. This kicked off a war of words most memorable for inciting Hilton's friend, the perpetually greasy trust fund baby Brandon Davis, to refer to Lohan as, among other things, a "firecrotch," and "really poor" for having a net worth of $7 million in a video that circulated as one of the first big hits for an in-its-infancy *TMZ*.

The advent of blogs like *TMZ* was one of several forces that changed celebrity media in the aughts. Tabloids had always done the big-game hunting of celebrity scandals, exposing affairs and drunk-driving charges, or whenever Russell Crowe was randomly screaming at someone, but in the mid-2000s, they took a new interest in daily mundanities—dry-cleaning runs and dog walking—that offered an unguarded look at people who were usually performing. Sensing that shift, editors at glossy magazines that once upon a time followed the leads of *Vogue* and *Women's Wear Daily*, publications that glamorized stars and emphasized their specialness, recognized an appetite for a different sort of celebrity coverage, one that could keep up with a twenty-four-seven news cycle and the increasingly snarky tone of the internet. In the spring of 2002, an insurgent *Us Weekly* editor named Bonnie Fuller was sifting through a stack of paparazzi photos for the week's issue and noticed one of Drew Barrymore picking up a penny on the sidewalk. It stood out to her as something readers might find novel, this elegant woman they knew from the big screen reaching down to the dirty sidewalk for spare change, so she put it in the magazine as a new feature: Stars—They're Just Like Us.

Dog walks and lunch breaks don't necessarily track as scandalous, but the tone of this style of coverage was about exposing the mirage of celebrity. Tabloids didn't need to uncover a crime or affair to act as though they were catching celebs in the act—the act of not being the sanctified gods and goddesses of the red carpets and runways they purported to be was more than enough. "Busted! Fast Food Fiends," a 2002 headline read. "For all their talk, you'd think celebrities subsist on celery sticks and Zone bars alone," went the copy, placed beneath images of an unsuspecting Jennifer Lopez shoving pizza in her mouth, Tom Cruise and Penélope Cruz skulking inside a Johnny Rockets, and Renée Zellweger exiting Koo Koo Roo slurping a soda with a bag of takeout in hand. Reese Witherspoon and Jake Gyllenhaal were shown at Coachella having "stacked their plates sky high with food" to "pig out." (The accompanying photos show Reese carrying two containers of salad and a Thai coconut, but whatever.)

Exposing the tricks celebrities used to craft unrealistically perfect images had value, and it could also be deliciously juicy. But this coverage also often preyed on audiences' worst instincts. It relied heavily on stereotypes, often racist or misogynistic ones, to shape narratives. It justified invasions of privacy by media outlets and reckless behavior by the paparazzi chasing down subjects, all in the name of feeding the thirst to see the Have-It-Alls taken down a notch. And it made *everything,* from dry-cleaning runs to nights out, a possible story.

For the crème de la crème of Hollywood cover stars—Gwyneth, Renée, Nicole—the reaction to this era was to hide. At their level of fame and prestige, getting your name in the papers was mostly a downside. This was especially true of women—groups of male stars, like the Leonardo DiCaprio–Tobey Maguire–Lukas Haas–Kevin Connolly "pussy posse," as it came to be known, could gallivant about town without much consequence, but for their female counterparts it was best to be seen only on red carpets and in the pages of *Vogue.* Perhaps because of this, another type of star became the obsession of tabloid media. She was one whose notoriety and public ubiquity was so entangled with her fame that she could never disappear on them. She was, as they called her, the It Girl.

It Girls came in various shapes (though not many sizes) and ilks—the East Coast variety trended sophisticated, full of media and fashion types like Tinsley Mortimer and Olivia Palermo, who spent their days toting Balenciaga City bags between runway shows and hawking their guest-edited collections for Bluefly.com or other early direct-to-consumer brands. The West Coast set was mostly former child stars and the wannabe-famous children of moguls, decked out for Starbucks runs in low-slung jeans or terrycloth tracksuits—the Mischa Bartons, Lauren Conrads, Tara Reids, and Nicole Richies. (The Olsen twins were a West Coast subcategory unto themselves, but at least they dressed well.) What they had in common is that they were all young, hot, and out on the town, inspiring metric tons of coverage of their nightly exploits that was simultaneously deeply invasive and usually provoked. "The night-clubs of LA are like soap operas," Richie wrote in her 2005 roman à clef, *The Truth About Diamonds,* which included a sixteen-page color photo spread of Richie on various escapades. "There's always some bizarre drama that plays out every night, and everyone in the cast—I mean, everyone—is great looking, stoned, and/or drunk." But Britney, Paris, and Lindsay were the three It Girls who had people rapt above the rest, the mononyms fixed at the center of the tabloid vortex.

In the mid-aughts tabloid heyday, barely an hour went by without a new cascade of news about the world's most famous twentysome-things. Nasty, juicy, and constant, media in the pre-influencer days had outsized power to train a spotlight on every minute of life inside the thirty-mile zone, the showbiz name for the chunk of greater Los Angeles encompassing much of the entertainment industry, and the inspiration for the name *TMZ*. The three women at the Hilton that night—Britney, Paris, and Lindsay—have each stood for the era's particular brand of notoriety and have also come to define the ways in which it ran out of control.

The months around the "Bimbo Summit" in November 2006 represent this era's peak in intensity—it was just three months later, in February 2007, that Britney Spears would shave her head in a public meltdown that has become another symbol of the times. Since then, the experiences of these women have forced a reckoning over tabloid culture that has changed the way we consider celebrity, and most significantly, the way professional media interacts with all celebrities, especially pop stars.

How those three came to share the front seat of Hilton's car on that November night gets fuzzy in the 2006 of it all—Spears was there because she'd become fast going-out friends with Hilton when she was newly single following her divorce from Kevin Federline. Hilton has since claimed that Lohan simply followed her into the car and she didn't want to kick her out. Her publicist—a onetime confidant of John Lennon named Elliot Mintz who, by the mid-aughts, spent his nights hovering near Hilton at parties and clubs, his garish suits and orange tan often visible in the corners of her photos—said he arranged for Hilton to give Lohan a ride home. Mintz's account seems the most reliable since he had a motive: Earlier that same evening, Lohan had approached a group of cameramen waiting for her in a parking garage and told them that Hilton had recently hit her, so their meeting was taken as a photo op intended to make things look copacetic. However they came to be squeezed into the car that night, the image became the ultimate symbol of the tabloid era run amok.

Lohan's path to the Beverly, and to It Girldom in general, was a rocky one. Just a few years earlier, she seemed to be on a different path, one toward a more glamorous form of traditional silver screen stardom. The little redhead from Long Island got her first modeling contract and was shooting Calvin Klein Kids ads before she was three. When she was eleven, she skipped school to beat out nearly four thousand other girls for the right to inhabit Nancy Meyers interiors on two separate continents in *The Parent Trap*, the iconic remake of the 1961 classic in which Lohan played twin sisters who scheme to get their divorced parents back together. That role catapulted Lohan into a slew of Disney Pictures movies including *Life-Size* (2000), *Get a Clue* (2002), *Freaky Friday* (2003), and *Confessions of a Teenage Drama Queen* (2004). Then, she did *Mean Girls*.

It seemed like she was on her way to A-list status as a movie star. I think the messiness that actually came next makes this easy to forget, but Lohan had sky-high expectations placed on her as an actress. In the eighties, there had been leading turns for women in major studio movies like Diane Keaton in *Annie Hall* or Meryl Streep in *Sophie's Choice*, but by the mid-aughts, they'd grown rare. In 2005, *The New York Times* reported that "not a single female-driven drama was a financial blockbuster." As the decade wore on, even the rom-coms that made superstars of Julia Roberts and Reese Witherspoon became increasingly bro-centric, replaced with Judd Apatow flicks and sex comedies like *Wedding Crashers*. The only movie in the top-ten highest grossing of the year to feature an actress in a leading turn was *Mr. & Mrs. Smith*. *Mean Girls* wasn't a drama, but it was so sharp, it had a female perspective, and Lohan was the glue that held it together. When she was cast in *A Prairie Home Companion* alongside Streep, people made comparisons between the two women and meant them.

To have followed down this path would have required maintaining the relatively refined public presence—one strategically doled out through *Vogue* covers and *Women's Wear Daily* interviews, not late nights in front of paparazzi—necessary to make a young lady seem "deserving" of that kind of fame in the way that someone like Streep, or Renée Zellweger, who often spoke about the lengths she went to control her profile, like avoiding autograph lines or spending less time in California. Unfortunately, while she was making *Mean Girls,* Lohan instead moved to LA to live with her boyfriend—you guessed it—Wilmer Valderrama. Her parents, with three other kids and their own issues, stayed home. (Lohan's father, Michael, was a screwup Wall Street trader who spent time in jail for securities fraud, an attempted assault, and a DUI.) Lindsay was young, had money to spend, and was desperate to be part of the in crowd and have a real social life for the first time ever. So she became friends with Hilton and entered the tabloid party scene.

It got messy fast. Lohan was still a Disney star and was filming *Herbie Fully Loaded,* and magazines started castigating her for being a child star who was out and about behaving like an adult. One of Lohan's first "scandals" was an icky drama over whether she'd gotten breast implants. A couple parents' groups had threatened to boycott *Herbie* because they found Lohan an inappropriate star for a kids movie, citing her clothes and the size of her boobs. The *New York Post* even claimed Lohan's breasts were digitally shrunk in the movie and that she was taken off the main posters for Herbie to minimize her appearance. Interviewers were not shy about asking Lohan deeply invasive questions. "I would never get a boob job," she told the *New York Daily News.* "I just wear fantastic Victoria's Secret bras." In June 2004, she auctioned off a signed bra, supposedly hers, for charity on eBay for $10,001. Then *Herbie* bombed at the box office and the movie's backers wound up whining it was her fault. "Celebrity is the enemy of stardom," president of Disney Pictures Nina Jacobson told *The New York Times* at the time. "Lindsay is so talented, but celebrity takes a lot of promising talent out of the mix. The public knows which stars pursue celebrity to feed their own ego and narcissism."

It's absolutely true that Lohan had started to go out a lot more, and that she was growing up in other ways. She was in a series of car accidents between 2004 and 2006, at least one of which was caused by a paparazzo who hit her while chasing down a photo. Her weight and health were observed intensely; she'd later reveal that she was struggling with bulimia. She was also working like crazy. Lohan had musical abilities, and her mom Dina Lohan had been throwing the idea of a pop album around for years. At one point there was a supposed record deal to write music with Emilio and Gloria Estefan that never went anywhere. She'd sung in movies—her *Freaky Friday* character Anna is one half of the fictional girl band Pink Slip, and at the end of the movie, Lohan performs "Ultimate" while making goo-goo eyes at Chad Michael Murray. She sang the theme for *Confessions*. *Mean Girls* used Lohan's singing voice, too—the Plastics could never have gotten through "Jingle Bell Rock" a cappella without her.

While she was filming *Herbie,* Lohan signed a deal with Tommy Mottola's Casablanca Records. Almost immediately, she started working on an album with John Shanks and Kara DioGuardi writing and producing, aiming for something "somewhere along the lines of hip-hop and rock." Lohan signed in July 2004, and her album *Speak* came out five months later, after a brief delay when she, balancing long days filming *Herbie,* studio time, and increasingly hard-partying, checked into Cedars-Sinai Medical Center with exhaustion. *Speak* did eventually go platinum, but it wasn't a major hit. Reviews called it a "mannered cash-in" and a "giant market researched disaster." I think that's a bit harsh, but the best argument for the album basically starts and ends with the song "Rumors," on which Lohan addresses her relationship with the press.

"Rumors" is an everybody-to-the-floor dance banger, a song about being so pissed off that everyone's gossiping about how much you party that all there's left to do is party some more. The strings give drama, the raspy quality in Lohan's voice communicates real anger, which makes her sound like someone who's spent the last several hours shouting over club music. The verses have an R&B feel that sets the scene—*Saturday, steppin' into the club*—of a night out that becomes progressively claustrophobic as Lohan feels sets of unwanted eyes trained on her. They groove methodically until the chorus, when she can't take it anymore. She's sick of rumors starting, she's sick of being followed. She's tired of people lying and saying what they want about her.

That "Rumors" chorus goes pretty hard. You can tell there's some actual rage there. It's not a soul-bearing kind of anthem—Lohan's basic problem with the paps in "Rumors" is that they're stopping her from getting fucked up and partying—but that's what's honest about it. She just wanted everyone to let her live! The music video tells the same story, an all-night odyssey of LiLo evading hordes of paparazzi by punching out hidden cameras and sending them chasing decoy cars (license plate: Lin Z) while she sneaks away to dance, let loose, and make out with some dude on a couch. She looks great. I think she's wearing a BumpIt. "Rumors," unfortunately, is about where the Lindsay Lohan story starts to become a bit of a bummer. She moved into the Chateau Marmont, and her next few years were more defined by feuds, arrests (for DUIs and shoplifting), and rehab stints than meaningful work. And she was constantly falling in and out with Hilton, whose frenemiship led both of them to the Hilton that night.

Unlike Lohan, Hilton was always a creature of places like the Beverly. Infamy came naturally to her. Before there were influencers, Hilton prototyped a kind of fame for fame's sake we're far more used to now thanks in no small part to her. Hilton got famous as the heiress to the hotel chain fortune, and she spent her early twenties hawking baby graphic tees from LA boutique Kitson and helping inspire the day's regrettably ubiquitous chunky highlights. She was an early reality TV participant, too—*The Simple Life* introduced viewers to many of the characters in her day-to-day orbit. That included her assistant at the time, Kim Kardashian, now her best present-day allegory. Hilton had a canny sense that you could make a lot of money just because people liked watching you live your life, and a lot of people did watch. For the most part she courted this attention, frequently calling the paparazzi on herself, leaning into drama and going out in photo-friendly Kitson tees with printed phrases like "Don't Be Jealous," "Too Pretty For a Job," and, of course, "That's Hot!" Still, she wasn't always in control of her own narrative. In 2004, an ex-boyfriend sold copies of what was supposed to be a private tape of himself and Hilton having sex. By 2006, she was the most googled person on the planet.

Around the same time, Hilton, like Lohan, turned to music as a way of commenting on her high profile. In 2005, she showed up to the VMAs with the producer Scott Storch on her arm. Storch was arguably the day's biggest name in hip-hop and R&B, despite being a white Jewish guy from Long Island who kind of looks like Pitbull (if Pitbull were a white Jewish guy from Long Island).

At the risk of underselling him, Storch has lived an interesting life—he was a child piano whiz who dropped out of high school as a freshman to play weddings and bar mitzvahs. By 1991, when he was eighteen, he'd moved to Philadelphia, fathered a son, and became the founding keyboard player in the Roots, the influential neo-soul group that's now the house band for Jimmy Fallon. After two albums, Storch realized he was more interested in producing than playing and left the band but continued to work with them as a writer, including on 1999's "You Got Me," a collaboration with Erykah Badu and the rapper Eve that became one of the band's biggest hits.

Eve really liked Storch, and she said as much to Dr. Dre, who promptly hired him to play keys and produce on his 1999 comeback album *2001*. If you've heard the song "Still D.R.E.," then you've heard a Storch beat. Those ominous, plunky eighth notes that serve as the intro? That's Storch on the keys. He became in demand after that and began a remarkable run of hitmaking: "Let Me Blow Ya Mind" for Eve; "Fighter" for Christina Aguilera; "Run It!" for Chris Brown; "Candy Shop" for 50 Cent; "Let Me Love You" for Mario; and "Cry Me a River" for—sigh—Justin Timberlake. It's Scott Storch's name that the rapper Fat Joe calls out in the intro of "Lean Back," 2004's song of the summer that popularized the "rockaway" dance.

Coming off that run is when Storch started partying with Paris Hilton. Fair warning, the Scott Storch story is about to get completely bananas. In 2005, Storch was living in Miami when he was introduced to Hilton by a mutual friend, Fereidoun "Prince Fred" Khalilian. At the time, Prince Fred was Hilton's partner in one of her latest ventures, the nightclub Club Paris. The two were spending a lot of time together in Miami where she was filming National Lampoon's *Pledge This!*, a movie I'm embarrassed to admit I have seen twice. Though his dealings with Hilton were uneventful, at least by Miami club standards, Khalilian turned out to be a con man who spent most of the aughts posing as a Middle Eastern royal in order to meet, work with, and profit off the fame of people like Hilton and Storch. He spent much of the next two decades having run-ins with the Federal Trade Commission over various fraudulent schemes until 2023, when he was arrested by the FBI for ordering a hit on a documentary filmmaker who was working on a project about him. He got caught because he had been duped by his body-guard, who he'd hired to murder the filmmaker but who instead staged a photo of the completed hit for Khalilian, then turned him in. Khalilian was eventually arrested inside a Las Vegas Dunkin' Donuts.

Anyway, Hilton was excited to meet Storch. She knew he was a producer, and she was having trouble with an album she was supposed to be working on. She'd decided she wanted to make an album and in 2004 established her own label, Heiress Records, but got wrapped up in a fight over the song "Screwed" with Haylie Duff, who claimed that Kara DioGuardi and Greg Wells had written it for her, not Hilton. After that, Hilton had a deal with the Black Eyed Peas and Lil Jon to make a record that I truly wish had happened just so we could hear what it would have sounded like, but they'd made no progress in part because Hilton was always in Miami. So when she hit it off with Storch, they got in the studio.

At the VMAs, Storch vouched for Hilton's seriousness to get the project done: "She's doing her thing and, I mean, the stuff is surprising," he said. "Every song we do now is like, totally amazing. We've got different style records, from serious, heartfelt rock songs to club-oriented, sing-along, hot records. It's balanced." I'm really tickled that Scott Storch was out there selling the "balance" of the Paris Hilton album with a straight face, but maybe that's what the aviators are for, and the man makes a good pitch.

The best part of *Paris*—originally titled *Paris Is Burning* before someone thought better of it—is that it's not balanced at all. It's thirty-nine minutes of light club fluff ending with a truly deranged cover of Rod Stewart's "Do Ya Think I'm Sexy." Hilton ran up the bill on industry veteran songwriters and producers: Along with Storch and DioGuardi, a young Dr. Luke was also among the credits for the album's second single "Nothing in This World." A lot of the reviews of *Paris* noted that the album was well-constructed, which figures given the number of pros involved. The *Los Angeles Times* said it "wasn't truly awful"; *Entertainment Weekly* liked the hooks but found the lyrics "often both inane and vaguely porny." That's a pretty good description of "Stars Are Blind," the lead single that got as high as number eighteen on the Hot 100.

"Stars Are Blind" is preposterously stupid. It is kind of a reggae song, which Paris obviously has no business singing. It's nominally a song about having sex, where Paris says to a guy *if you show me real love, baby, I'll show you mine,* a line that seems not *not* about her sex tape, which would be rather dark subject material. Really, though, "Stars Are Blind" is about Paris Hilton. It's not so much that the story is about her, but the performance of it is both blithely dumb and a tiny bit winking in a way that only Hilton could really pull off. She says the words "nice and naughty" a lot, and she's excited about that. It makes sense that Hilton's music was less aggrieved than a song like "Rumors" was, since Hilton courted scandal in a way that Spears and Lohan didn't. That's a little bit of the magic, too—listening to someone luxuriating in the same spotlight that had exposed her.

After *Paris,* Hilton maintained a passing interest in music. She DJs. In 2024, she released another album, *Infinite Icon,* that was tracking to debut high on the *Billboard* albums chart before surprisingly missing the chart altogether, usually a sign that an artist is suspected of buying up all their own records. But her first record did not signal a new career direction for her—*Paris* was really just something she could do while she did her real job of being Paris Hilton. The actual person for whom *Paris* marked an inflection point was Storch, who, around the time he dated and worked with Hilton, became about as expensively self-destructive as one can be with $100 million and a coke problem.

That summer of 2006 marked a peak in Storch's infamy when news reports claimed he had spent $30 million on a stash of cocaine that lasted him six months. He was a conspicuous consumer—he bought a yacht and a jet and at least twenty luxury cars, many of them purchased while high. He had a penchant for ridiculous celebrity interactions—Storch once invited Questlove to dinner with O. J. Simpson, where Simpson pitched that the Roots write a song defending his honor (Questlove declined). You can see where this is going: The natural conclusions of bankruptcy and rehab were both reached by 2009, and Storch's days as a hitmaker were pretty much done. Hilton's, too.

Spears, obviously, didn't need a circuitous path to music. But between herself, Lohan, and Hilton, her journey to tabloid It Girl-dom was probably the most reluctant. She was less of a partier in general, and earlier bouts of tabloid coverage of Britney tended to revolve around her romantic relationships. There was the breakup drama with Justin Timberlake in 2002, her fifty-five-hour marriage to Jason Allen Alexander in 2004, her marriage to Kevin Federline later that year and their divorce and subsequent custody battle in 2007. Spears had been struggling with her mental health for years by that point, but it was after then that her public behavior became noticeably strange and erratic and a major focus of the tabloids.

By late 2006, she hadn't released a full studio album in three years, since 2003's In the Zone. Spears had been saying since November 2003 that she was working on her fifth album, but there had been delays, and Spears had taken some time off to have two children. Jive, though, was running out of greatest hits releases, remix collections, and K-Fed collaborations they could package to keep the money train on the tracks, and in the spring of 2006 Britney got back to the studio in earnest. On the night of the "Bimbo Summit," she was in the midst of recording her album Blackout, ultimately created and released during the peak of her fame and the most tumultuous period of her life.

Blackout is an album of excellent, impersonal dance music. Its first single was "Gimme More," the song that gave us the iconic intro "It's Britney, bitch." But right after introducing herself, Spears's voice gets modulated to an unrecognizable point, submerged in producer Danja's robotic beats. There are no ballads, and the album marked the start of a trend in Spears's records in which her voice became less and less central to the music. That is not to say she made no impact—for the first time in her career, Spears was an executive producer on *Blackout* and by many accounts deeply involved in the album's creation. It's an exceptional piece of music, and it goes down as a canny foray into EDM just before it started to boom all across pop music. But without knowing those things, just by hearing the album, there's very little way of telling it belongs to Britney Spears. Except, that is, for "Piece of Me."

Because Spears's personal life was in a tenuous spot, producers working on her upcoming album were told by her label not to write about it. Clapping back, in particular, was off-limits—Jive had rejected the Cathy Dennis song "Sweet Dreams My LA Ex" for *In the Zone* because it was a response to "Cry Me a River," and the songwriters working with Spears on her fifth album, *Blackout,* knew they weren't to attempt anything similar.

But with the album nearly finished—this would have been late 2006—Swedish production duo Bloodshy & Avant wanted to bend the rules. They'd had a smash with Britney already—Bloodshy & Avant produced "Toxic"—and felt like they had some leeway, plus they'd been around her enough by that point to know what a major part of her life dealing with the tabloid press had become. En route to a prior recording session, they'd had a scary experience driving with Spears when the paparazzi descended at high speed. It was memorable, and they wanted to write about it.

The song that came out of that impulse, "Piece of Me," was the last song recorded for *Blackout*. I think it's the best of Spears's entire career. It's an electro-pop manifesto about what it means to be chewed up into newspaper pulp that serves as one of the clearest statements of her experience in one of the darker stretches of her life. Over and over in the song, Spears, maybe flirting, maybe threatening, asks, *you want a piece of me?!* Her voice is synthesized and pitch-shifted to the high heavens, an intentional trick, but there are stretches of the song's verses—*I'm miss bad media karma, another day another drama*—when she's the only thing you hear.

It's pretty compelling, hearing her spell out the laundry list of lose-lose scenarios she's lived. The public's experience with Spears at that point included a lot of grainy videos of her getting in and out of cars, body blocked by security, trying as hard as possible *not* to be observed, and this was a song about her in her voice. "Piece of Me" was essential, so it was made the second single for *Blackout* and allowed on the record despite the personal content. Its Hot 100 peak was number eighteen, but over time it's become one of the bestselling singles of Spears's career.

"Piece of Me" would have been recorded right around the "Bimbo Summit." In hindsight, it was the tipping point when the tabloid era Spears, Lohan, and Hilton touched on musically got completely, obviously out of control. Within just a few months, Spears would shave her head and Lohan would be arrested in the first of two drug- and alcohol-related arrests that year. Paris, too, had a run-in with the law. She had been arrested in September 2006 on suspicion of a DUI while driving to In-N-Out Burger—Hilton said she'd had one margarita on an empty stomach—but pleaded down to reckless driving, getting three years' probation and a fine. But she was pulled over again in May 2007 for speeding, driving without headlights, and violating the terms of her probation agreement. She was sentenced to forty-five days in jail. Her sentencing caused a stir—a "Break Paris out of Jail" Flash game made the rounds online, where the player would run around as Paris in a jumpsuit, searching for keys while avoiding the gaze of guards or trying to jump high enough on a trampoline to clear the gates and escape. Hilton herself promoted a fan petition that appealed for her pardon to then California governor Arnold Schwarzenegger. It read, "if the late former president Gerald Ford could find it in his heart to pardon former president Richard Nixon after his mistake(s) . . ." then Paris deserved the same. (I have to say, I absolutely love the optional plural on that.) Ultimately, Paris served three days in jail and then was transferred to house arrest for the remainder of her sentence.

Britney's and Lindsay's situations continued to be darker. Lohan went in and out of various rehabs eight times. She struggled with addiction and eating disorders. Her career floundered for a long time. Spears's struggles, which stemmed from her separation from her children, the sudden death of a beloved aunt, and the constant pursuit of the press, led her family to place her under a legal conservatorship, which they used to control her for over a decade. Spears's fight to dissolve that conservatorship was ultimately successful in November 2021, prompting a slew of long-form print and documentary-style media coverage that told her story and revisited the tabloid era with fresh eyes. Spears was the subject of Netflix's *Britney vs Spears*, FX and *The New York Times'* *Controlling Britney Spears*, and CNN's *Toxic: Britney Spears' Battle for Freedom*. The tone was almost entirely sympathetic, and collectively, these series read as a referendum on an earlier era, on the dangerous practices of paparazzi and the invasive tendencies of the tabloids that preyed on women like Spears and drove them to the brink.

Spears's conservatorship was dissolved right around the fifteen-year anniversary of the "Bimbo Summit," which served as an occasion to revisit the arcs of Paris and Lindsay, too. It helped that things were looking good for the gals: Just that month, each member of the unholy trinity had reached a milestone that was wholesome instead of tawdry. Hilton had just gotten married to a venture capitalist named Carter Reum in Bel Air wearing Oscar de la Renta; beyond wedding planning she'd been spending time on Capitol Hill advocating for policy intended to prevent the same types of abuse she'd experienced at a boarding school in her teens. Lohan had recently announced her acting comeback in the Netflix holiday rom-com *Falling for Christmas*. Spears, after thirteen years of silence, was legally back in control of her finances, personal life, and medical decisions; she was also soon to be married to longtime boyfriend Sam Asghari.

The upshot of all that coverage seemed to suggest that things have gotten better, all around—better for these women in their lives and better in a culture that's less inclined to chew them up and spit them out. Some of this celebration was a bit premature—a few years after the bimbo-versary, Hilton seems to be doing well, and Lohan has settled into motherhood and making Netflix rom-coms, but Spears remains at odds with her family, has divorced from Asghari, and often posts concerning videos on social media. And some of this celebration was just a bit too self-congratulatory. I remember hearing the phrase "regained her narrative" a lot to describe projects about people who declined to participate in them and seemed to wish they didn't exist.

So then, what's the impact of the "Bimbo Summit" and its fallout on how we now see stars and pop stars? While I think as a culture, we've arrived at a place where we recognize the importance of reflecting on what these female celebrities endured, to me, the true reckoning over the tabloid culture of the aughts was with the behavior of professional media. Tabloids are always gonna tabloid, but the *Us Weekly*s and *Star Magazine*s and even *Page Six*es aren't anywhere near as nasty as they once were. As of this writing, the most recent Stars—They're Just Like Us mostly used photos from celebrities' Instagram pages—"They Read the Menu!" read the caption below a photo of Snooki eating dinner with her kids. The single true paparazzi photo in the bunch was of Jeremy Allen White buying flowers at a Los Angeles farmer's market, which he seems to do every day. Pretty tame. The cattiest bloggers of the day, too, from Perez Hilton to *Lainey Gossip*'s Elaine Lui, have been brought to heel and made many public apologies, particularly around the time the Britney docs led to wide public discussion of how the nastiness of their coverage had real impact. To be clear, this is good—there were established norms around certain media behaviors, including high-speed car chases by thirsty photographers sanctioned by the magazines that bought their photos, that not only became considered widely invasive but extremely dangerous. Over the course of working on this book, I talked to many people who lived and worked in Hollywood around this time, and almost all of them said something along the lines of "it was even worse than you think." No one said the opposite was true.

Now, that does not mean everything now is sunshine and roses! Catty, tawdry coverage still exists, but it tends to come from different, and less officially sanctioned places. Rumors start on Deuxmoi and in Reddit threads. Snark comes from random Twitter users. It is also not correct to say that every tendency of mid-aughts celeb coverage was wrong and harmful. The impulse to puncture the illusion of glossy magazine profiles was a good one, and even those magazines were less automatically accommodating to the celebrity PR machine than they are today. Also, many of the celebrities who were exploited by the paparazzi and tabloids exploited them right back—Hilton is a prime example. But the reckoning over tabloid media coverage has created the expectation that professionals in the press treat celebrities more gently than they did in the aughts. Laws have restricted the ability of paparazzi to go after the children of celebrities—something that certainly would have helped Britney Spears in her day. Magazines simply spend a lot less time plainly calling people fat, ugly, and crazy, and I think we can all agree that is for the best.

These changes apply to all celebrities, but I do think they have special resonance for pop stars. Britney obviously came by it honestly, but I don't think it's a coincidence that Paris and Lindsay made their forays into pop stardom at the peak of their tabloid exposure. It works because pop stardom is the showbiz job where the character you play is yourself, and through their music, these women were commenting on a particular brand of celebrity in which their inner lives were always on full display. Fans of Charli XCX—or for that matter, Kim Kardashian's "Jam (Turn It Up)"— know the It Girl/pop star pipeline has remained strong. And the women of the "Bimbo Summit" have been canonized therein. Britney is obviously in a slightly different category, but "Stars Are Blind" and "Rumors" have lived on as totems of their era, too. I've seen both referred to as "cult hits," reliably in rotation at gay bars or as millennial bait. To me, they're songs you put on kind of as a bit before they work their way into you and you wind up texting someone, *Remember "Rumors"? That shit slaps.* More recent generations of pop stars seem to feel the same. In 2023, Hilton rereleased a version of "Stars Are Blind" with the pop star Kim Petras. In 2019, Miley Cyrus popped up singing "Rumors" karaoke style on her

Instagram Story, tagging Lohan, which led to a sweet back-and-forth. For Halloween in 2022, the girl band Muna did a show in costume as Pink Slip; the members have also brought up their love of Lohan in interviews. " 'Rumors' is one of the most underrated songs of all time," guitarist Naomi McPherson told *Pitchfork* in an interview in 2023. As with all these songs, it's an artifact of a not-too-distant past, when celebrity culture consumed a significant amount of popular art—and threatened to consume the artists themselves. Increasingly, it seems, it's a message many can agree on: *Can't we just let them live?*

8

How Taylor Swift Invented the Internet

PLEASE BEAR WITH ME, BECAUSE I AM GOING TO TRY TO describe a Myspace page from 2005. The background is a salmon-y shade of orange; the profile picture is of a blond girl with curly hair looking over her shoulder. The posts themselves are photos of the girl and her friends, plus an enthusiastically posed selfie from an early-gen MacBook Photo Booth app. The sepia filter seems to be a favorite, as is the one meant to make photos look like comic book drawings by putting weird lines over everything, which was always great for masking acne scars. Black and white is reserved for moody solo shots, of course. The written posts are peppered with inside jokes and references to crushes and school dances in AIM chat-speak.

12 Oct 2005 4:13
Everybody watch Kelsey's scrolling pictures of her friends until you get to the one of shelby.

Her boobs look AMAZING.

Hahahahahahaha

28 Dec 2005 2:57 PM

Just a little reminder to you that, even though the semester
may be over..

I'm still quite obsessed with you.

haha fuck sewing machines.

lovelovelove

-T-

4 Feb 2006 9:01 PM

THAT PICTURE OF ME UP AT THE TOP IS GROSS.

THAT IS SICK TAKE IT DOWN.

It serves NO purpose other than to make me look FUGLY.

I want it off NOW.

but i loove you

You have probably realized by now that I am writing about Taylor Swift's Myspace page. (*It serves NO purpose other than to make
me look FUGLY*—the original *so casually cruel in the name of being
honest.*) The posts are artifacts from Swift's days at Hendersonville
High School in Nashville, Tennessee, where she moved in eighth
grade when her family relocated to support her budding career as a
country singer-songwriter. Many years later Swift would explain
that, when she writes, she thinks of her compositions in one of
three pens: fountain pen for deeply personal confessions like "All
Too Well," quill pen for the dreamy stylizations that populate *Folklore* and *Evermore,* and glitter gel pen for frivolous fun like "Shake
It Off," but these posts are best read in the lingua franca of a teenager alone with her peers in a world of their own creation. The

clumsy wing-womaning, the performative hinting at inside jokes, the use of "fugly"—it's the obvious signature of a young millennial navigating the digital equivalent of a high school cafeteria.

In a twist of Web 2.0–era fate, the day after Swift created her Myspace page, a former DreamWorks record executive named Scott Borchetta signed the papers to form his new indie label, Big Machine Label Group. Borchetta knew of Swift because when she was fourteen he'd seen her perform at The Bluebird Cafe, a storied Nashville venue for scouting talent, during a writer's night (get-in price: eight dollars) and found himself charmed by this ambitious teenager with a tendency toward TMI. Now running his own shop, Borchetta made Swift one of Big Machine's first signings. When they released her debut single, "Tim McGraw," in June 2006, the label was still so new that Swift and her mother Andrea sat on the floor for hours—they had yet to buy furniture—packaging hundreds of CDs to send off to radio stations.

There is so much of present-day Taylor in "Tim McGraw." The melody, the storytelling, and the marketing genius are all there in this tuneful ode to young love Swift wrote while zoning out in math class before polishing up in a fifteen-minute session with songwriter Liz Rose. It's not fair to say that in those three minutes it's possible to discern the alchemy of factors that, twenty years later, have led to Paul McCartney handing out friendship bracelets at her shows or presidential candidates begging for her endorsements, but the bones are there. This book is about the artists of the 2000s, and when I was conceiving the chapters, I thought about whether to include Swift. On the one hand, she began her career then and released multiple huge albums in that first decade she was working. I, however, don't think of her canonically as a 2000s artist; the work she'll be most remembered for, from "All Too Well" to the mega pop hits of *1989* to owning the pandemic with *Folklore* and

Evermore or to the world-dominating power of Taylor's Versions and The Era's Tour, happened in the 2010s and 2020s. Maybe two more decades from now she'll have redefined herself *again*. But when I think of Swift in the *context* of the aughts and ask myself to define the legacy of her 2000s work, what I come up with does have a lot to do with where she—and the entire state of pop music—is now. It was in this era that Swift wrote the blueprint for modern standom and began developing her fan base, in concert with the rise of social media, into a hugely powerful tool. Both a defining feature and a power source for modern pop stardom is the relationship between the artist and their online fan base, and I would argue Taylor Swift has the single biggest hand in creating that dynamic.

There weren't a lot of fourteen-year-olds on country radio, nor were there a lot of women, so name-checking the biggest star in Nashville in a tune about a girl hoping a former beau will remember her fondly when he hears her favorite song was pretty savvy. Still, getting airplay was an uphill battle. In an *EW* interview in 2008, Swift's manager, Rick Barker, described the campaign to get "Tim McGraw" on the radio. "Radio does research," he said. "And we have no idea who they're researching, but it was saying people weren't digging 'Tim McGraw.'"

This simply couldn't have been right. While the song was meeting resistance from radio, Swift's social following was modest but growing, in the tens of thousands (she had thirty-four thousand friends as of November 2006). And those followers loved "Tim McGraw." Music was big on Myspace—users could share playlists; everyone got to pick a signature song that would auto-play whenever anyone visited their profile, and it was seeming like there were a lot of users who liked presenting themselves alongside this sharp young woman with gorgeous curls who was putting stories about their lives and their concerns at the center of her songs. They might have lacked the volume of radio, but a grassroots movement was building around the song and around Swift, who was just as native to Myspace as any of the users who were discovering her on it.

When the song started to gain traction, Swift blogged on her page that she wanted to thank any radio stations that were playing "Tim McGraw" and asked followers to comment where they'd heard it. Even a station that was playing "Tim McGraw" only once a week in the middle of the night might have had a programmer answer the phone to find Swift herself on the other line, relaying the positive feedback. It became her own form of market research, a counterargument to the radio surveys that had underestimated the song. "We were able to take those moments back to radio in individual markets and say, 'You're saying research is telling you it's not doing that great, but here are eighty-five people who are telling us they love your station because you played 'Tim McGraw,' " Barker said. Myspace helped them demonstrate that Swift had an audience that did listen to the radio, but maybe it wasn't the group of people most likely to answer a survey call or be the head of household listed in the Whitepages. And that got stations to play the song.

Swift used her Myspace actively, a precursor to how she would engage with her fandom years later. She's always had a bit of Tracy Flick to her, and in those days, she corralled fans with the energy of an overachiever running for student council president. When Swift won the CMT Music Award for Breakthrough Video of the Year the following spring, she told every one of her supporters that her victory was theirs, too. "This is for my Myspace people and every-body who voted," she said in her speech. Backstage, she told inter-viewers that she was spending at least thirty minutes a day thanking

people who'd showed support for her online with individual comments. "I'm a junior in high school, this is how we campaign," she
said.

By then, Swift's debut album, *Taylor Swift*, was in the middle of
a slow, but fierce burn. It sold thirty-nine thousand copies in its
first week, good for a new artist, but it kept selling long after. The
album hit a million in sales by its first birthday and reached its peak
at number five on the *Billboard* 200 in January 2008. The album
wound up spending 157 weeks on the chart, the longest stay for
any US debut release in the 2000s. The Myspace listens rolled in
and "Tim McGraw," "Our Song," "Picture to Burn," and "Tear-
drops on My Guitar" all became country hits. Swift spent the summer as an opener for Rascal Flatts and joining Faith Hill and the
actual Tim McGraw on tour. Make no mistake, she was a country
artist making country music with country musicians, songwriters,
and producers for a Nashville label, but her nascent fan base had
more demographic overlap with a Top 40 audience than, say,
Brooks & Dunn. And in an early hint at what was to come, "Tear-
drops" got a music video that aired on *TRL* and a Top 40 remix,
which went all the way to Swift's lucky number thirteen—of course—
on pop radio.

It shouldn't have been a total shock that a songwriter who synthesized the angsts and joys of teenagers would have found an audience in 2006. This was my teen microgeneration, and those
really were some glory days for the young adult content industrial
complex. I'd arrive home from school to a new *That's So Raven* on
Mondays and *Hannah Montana* and *The Suite Life of Zack and
Cody* on Fridays. Weekends had *iCarly* on Saturdays and *Zoey 101*
on Sundays, and for anything in between, this was the high period
of the Disney Channel Original Movie. The library stocked dog-
eared copies of the Clique series, Cecily von Ziegesar's Gossip Girl

books, and Louise Rennison's Confessions of Georgia Nicholson series. In music, the *High School Musical* soundtrack was the bestselling album of 2006, and around the same time, a band of brothers from New Jersey (née: Jonas) had formed and were touring in support of Jesse McCartney, the Cheetah Girls, and Aly & AJ under the Disney/Hollywood Records orbit. This was the moment in which Taylor arrived—one where many young people, and especially young women, were voraciously consuming the stories of their own lives reflected back to them through their headphones and screens.

If you were part of this microgeneration, odds are good you spent a lot of time online. If I was home, the green "available" dot on my AIM screen (username: mangorainbow99) was reliably lit up. My friends and I would chat there for hours, far more intimately than we ever would have in person. The digital universe felt somehow less self-conscious than real life. My average answer if asked how I was doing in person would be something like "fine, thanks," while my average status update maxed out its character count in angsty pre–Tumblr poetry. The other thing I spent a lot of time doing on the internet was searching around for new music, both the thing that made me feel the biggest rush of joy and something that was beginning to twist itself into the backbone of my identity. I'd spend hours clicking through YouTube videos and listening to poorly named LimeWire files or ten-second iTunes Store previews, hunting for something I could get stuck in my head.

It was around this time, and in this way, that I discovered Taylor. Something that will bother me forever is the fact that despite the metric tons of information about this woman rattling around in my brain, I don't remember the exact moment that it happened, or what the first song of hers I ever heard was. I do know what hooked me, though—a bootleg copy of an unreleased song called "Perma-

nent Marker" that was kicking around YouTube. I can't say "Permanent Marker" is A-plus Swift, though it's pretty funny. The refrain
goes: X *is the shape I drew on your face in permanent marker, ohhhh
yeah!*

I loved the directness of "Permanent Marker." You've got to hand
it to her, that line does not pull any punches, it's just a sneering
Taylor Swift informing you she's going to go medieval on your
yearbook photo with a Sharpie. This was my favorite quality of
hers, the way her songs were completely scrutable. The characters in
her songs at least claimed to feel a shyness I could relate to—*if you
asked me if I love him, I'd lie* is the refrain of "I'd Lie," a song entirely
about saving face—but that never stopped her from saying exactly
what she was feeling in the course of the lyrics. Because of this, I
had a real affinity for the kiss-off tracks in her early discography,
songs with lines I could only dream of delivering so confidently.

You should've said no, you should've gone home!
I hate that stupid, old pickup truck you never let me drive!

I had no reason to say any of these things. No one was really
wronging me in 2006. I definitely couldn't drive. But I was (am)
rather sensitive, and isn't it the right of a young woman to feel just
a little bit wronged all the time, regardless of circumstance? And I
do think that even if I had real reason to stand up for myself I
would have had a hard time doing that. My sickest documented
burn during this era came during a sixth-grade science class (when
it was just "science") in which my classmates and I were tasked with
identifying and plotting the locations of several trees in the woods
behind our school building. (Do not ask me why we did this, all I
know is that it's impossible to write about the specifics of a liberal
arts education without sounding completely ridiculous.) Anyway, a

classmate of mine named Sarah, who I held a healthy skepticism toward stemming from a third-grade slumber party invitation that must have gotten lost in the mail, and who, let's face it, was being a little dramatic, expressed concern that we would hurt the trees by tying string around them in order to measure their distance from one another. Fed up with her antics, I had a rare moment of assertiveness: "We're not going to hurt them, Sarah," I said. "Trees don't have nervous systems."

This story is big in my family because it was very unusual for me to pipe up like that. It might be my mother's favorite story to retell, ever—I think to her, I momentarily transformed into a *Def Comedy Jam* comic. Though I will say, the last time she brought this story up she informed me that my memory of the slumber party incident is wrong, and that I was not harboring lasting resentment when I laid down the sharpest verbal barb of my young existence as I stood betwixt birch and spruce wearing various Limited Too fashions. To her memory, it was this spoken gauntlet that led to the slumber party incident. Which makes me the villain of this story! I don't remember it that way, but clearly I had a lot going on at the time.

Anyway, to a girl with big feelings in search of a vehicle to let them out, Swift was perfect. In her music, she always had a perfect line ready and while she felt rejection from cliques and boys, she always got the last laugh. We didn't talk about parasocial relationships with celebrities in those days, but she felt like a friend, both because she paid attention to fans and because she acted like a peer. She let you into her life by vlogging her days—posting selfie-style videos of herself and friends lip-synching to Katy Perry's "Hot 'n' Cold" or "Wannabe" by the Spice Girls interspersed with behind-the-scenes footage from shows and her life out on the road. The circumstances of her life weren't normal, but she was still a teenager—in one old vlog, Swift and her mom went to the dentist to get a replacement retainer because, as Andrea Swift chided, Taylor was always leaving hers in hotel rooms.

She was funny and over-the-top in an earnest way. When she played pickup basketball with her band, she shouted, "That's the best thing that's ever happened in my life!" after making a bucket. She seemed fun to be around, too. She baked cakes for her brother's birthday, went to see songwriter Liz Rose get married at a Vegas chapel, went bowling with Selena Gomez, who told the camera they were "homies hardcore," or goofed off with her fiddle player, Caitlin, by walking around backstage at a show staring pointedly at various other band members until they got weirded out and said something. And from her earliest days out on tour, she talked to audiences like they were close confidants whispering secrets back and forth. When she was out on the road opening for Kenny Chesney after the debut album cycle, she'd introduce the breakup kiss-off "Picture to Burn" with a special shout-out:

"Please know that I try to be a really nice person in general," she'd say as the band vamped the intro. "But if you break my heart, or if you hurt my feelings, or ANY OF MY FRIENDS FROM BAKERSFIELD, CALIFORNIA—well, I will have to write a song about you!"

And just like that, the entire audience was besties with Taylor Swift.

We didn't say "Swifties," yet, but being a fan of Taylor's was like belonging to a club—a club full of all your friends who loved and felt and longed in the same way. And any good club needs a club-house.

The World Wide Web went live on April 30—Taurus queen!—of 1993. Much of the online infrastructure that already existed, though, had been designed around fandom. In the 1970s, fans of the Grateful Dead from Silicon Valley, in particular, started some of the earliest internet affinity publications. The first digital bulletin board was called Community Memory, and it sprung up out of a Berkeley record store in 1973 so that a group of locals equally invested in the tech and counterculture scenes could discuss music and literature—but mostly the Grateful Dead. The same year, an artificial intelligence researcher named Paul Martin from Stanford created what was essentially an early listserv so that he and his buddies from the lab could streamline their frequent email conversations about the Dead. Two years later, he made that list semipublic with the help of ARPANET, the US Department of Defense's experimental communication network that was the forebearer of the modern internet.

For a long time, these were heavily male spaces. The earliest internet platforms were invite-only, and usage was reserved mostly for white men in the right networks to receive those invitations and who could afford the technology and service fees necessary to make use of them. Even as access widened, the assumption that online spaces were male spaces kept many women offline, or at the very least hidden when they were online. "There are no girls on the internet," a line that grew out of gaming communities in the nineties, is still a common catchphrase scrawled on bro-centric forums like Reddit or 4chan. It is also rule number thirty in the Rules of the Internet, a living document that circulates around a lot of the same channels. If rule number thirty establishes who is welcome online, rule number thirty-one establishes the standard response to anyone claiming to be female and logged-on at the same time: "tits or GTFO."

But as early as the 1990s, women on the internet were real, and they were spectacular. In 1994, the researchers Nancy Kaplan and Eva Farrell wrote an ethnography of "young women on the net," which pointed out that groups of teenage girls were some of the most participatory users of online bulletin boards that were owned and operated, and presumed mostly to be used, by men. Soon enough, those users were creating their own fan websites. The arrival of GeoCities, a user-generated website platform, after 1994 was another breakthrough; it made for the easy creation of clip-art-laden fan pages for the Backstreet Boys, *NSYNC, and Destiny's Child and for TV shows like *Buffy the Vampire Slayer* or *Dawson's Creek*. By 2000, women were getting online at faster rates than men according to a Pew Research Center study. Follow-up research in 2005 showed that 86 percent of American women between eighteen and twenty-nine were online, compared with 80 percent of their male counterparts. By the end of the decade, it wasn't just about who was *joining* the internet, there were simply more women online than men. This was especially true on social media. In 2009, 21 percent of American women online had Twitter accounts, but only 17 percent of men did.

The more women got online, the more it became apparent they wanted different things out of the experience than their male counterparts. Describing the teen enthusiasts populating the nineties message boards, Kaplan and Farrell wrote that the women wanted "to maintain connection rather than to convey information" when they posted. The Pew report described the new female users as "Instant Acolytes," who were generally more enthusiastic about the internet than male users because their "applications are as much social as transactions-oriented." The person they're describing sounds a lot like a fangirl.

When I hear the word "fangirl," I hear it with all its implied judgment and hysteria. But by any reasonable definition, I am one. My Spotify Wrapped data has never placed me outside the top 1 percent of highest-volume Taylor Swift listeners on the platform, which, according to a *Wall Street Journal* analysis, means I am listening to at least six thousand minutes per year. Even if I cut that in half—which feels conservative—to account for the fact that I imagine I spent less time listening in her early days when her catalog was not as deep—that means I have spent well over a month of my existence listening to her songs. And the bounds of my interest reach far beyond passive enjoyment. I'm part of no fewer than four group texts specifically devoted to talking about Taylor Swift, each of them named for a different Swiftie in-joke. ("Taylor Support Group," "Still Swift AF Boi," "Grab your [passport emoji] and my [hand emoji]," and "Free Dibbles"—IYKYK.) I have friends I've never met in person but feel genuinely close to because we talk about Taylor Swift together. I know song lyrics by heart, that Swift has had Lasik eye surgery, that her cat Meredith has an estimated net worth of $93 million, and after two glasses of Chablis I can make you a solid case that the album *1989* secretly tells the story of the time Swift and Harry Styles committed vehicular manslaughter together. I might balk at the label, but that's fangirldom.

Over the course of Swift's career, the general public has gotten more and more clued in to the power of the fangirl. That's partly because her base of supporters has grown, sure, but it's also because the fangirling (in the neither derogatory nor gendered sense) itself has moved out into the open, when it used to take place in relative private. In their early iterations, online fan spaces were, in fact, like clubhouses. Entry was either literally gatekept, or communities were still small and niche enough that you wouldn't wind up on a Phish message board—or a Spice Girls one—unless you really meant to be there. As the internet developed into the backbone of modern society—and before algorithms were actively siloing users by interest at the rate they do now—social media platforms became more like a town square where all different kinds of people came together, for better and for worse. The late 2000s and early 2010s, the era in which Swift became a star and established her audience, were peak years for the viral video. This was the time of the Ice Bucket Challenge or—less charitably—Chatroulette, the webcam site that paired random users together to videoconference. (Chatroulette had a huge moment in 2009 but was ruined almost immediately because it was completely overrun by penises.)

In these years, fan bases that had previously been relatively insular became more visible to outsiders. On the one hand, this gave fandoms a lot of power. In 2007, the year after Myspace helped Swift make her debut, the music manager Scooter Braun discovered a young Justin Bieber on the same platform and helped him become a superstar with a massive online fan base. In 2009, Rihanna fans migrated their online hub from a small blog co-run by a group of fans to the Twitter account @RihannaDaily and also gave themselves an official name: the Navy. Fan accounts for Beyoncé fans (the Beyhive) and Lady Gaga fans (the Little Monsters) also appeared that year. In 2010, Simon Cowell Frankensteined five boys, all individual contestants on the TV singing competition *The X Factor,* into the boy band One Direction, which for the five years following, was among the biggest acts in the world as much for their goofy social media presences as for their music. (While I am most tapped into the ways in which Swifties helped build the modern social internet, the author Kaitlyn Tiffany's wonderful book *Everything I Need I Get From You* does the same for One Direction fans, another pioneering group, and pointed me in the direction of several studies cited in this chapter.)

On the other hand, the more fandom began to operate out in the open, the more likely individual fan groups were to come into conflict with each other or with outsiders who didn't understand their jokes, references, or why they cared so much in the first place. Fangirls are easily misunderstood because they (we) are often kidding around *and deadly serious* at the same time. A Tweet like "If Taylor Swift kills me do NOT prosecute her. She caught ME slipping that's on ME," is at once intentionally absurd *and* an earnest expression of deep feelings of fandom. Anyone posting like that would likely be termed a "stan"—a portmanteau of "stalker" and "fan"—a term which emerged around the turn of the century, both from Eminem's 2000 song "Stan," about a deranged and obsessive fan, and from a line in Nas's Jay-Z diss track "Ether" in 2001. By the late 2000s and early 2010s, it was a common, and more benign, way to refer to enthusiastic fan bases—and a way they referred to themselves. Stans even developed their own somewhat condescending term for *non*-stans: locals, who stans consider to be those bland users who merely post the occasional pumpkin patch shot or status update and who are wholly dispassionate to the point of barely being alive. The chasm between the two is the space between feeling deeply about a celebrity you've never met and not understanding how that's even possible. It's wondering, *why do you care so much,* or *how could you not?*

The night of September 13, 2009—the night of the MTV Video Music Awards—arrived right at the outset of this period of fandoms adjusting to life in the open. By this time, Taylor Swift wasn't doing slow burns, or campaigning for handfuls of radio spins anymore. She also wasn't "just" a country star. Her second album *Fearless* had elevated her to a new level of fame and ubiquity thanks to singles "Love Story" and "You Belong with Me," which were pop radio hits. The album sat at number one for eight weeks and Swift wound up the bestselling artist of 2009. When tickets for the *Fearless* tour went live, she sold out the Staples Center in Los Angeles in two minutes. She was becoming a household name; she hosted *Saturday Night Live* and did bits with Ellen DeGeneres. She'd always had a habit of name-checking her boyfriends—or ex-boyfriends—in songs, but the relatively anonymous Drews and Stephens had been replaced by names people knew: Joe Jonas, a just-post-*Twilight* Taylor Lautner. She was collecting awards by the barrelful, and observers had begun to notice that she had a habit of making the same mouth-agape shocked face when her name was called for the umpteenth time. To some, the credibility with which she could sing underdog lines like *she's cheer captain and I'm on the bleachers* was waning since the cheer captain would probably incinerate her pompoms and ritually sacrifice the quarterback in exchange for a pair of concert tickets. To fans—and this is how I felt at the time—the kinship with her was so strong that *our* perspectives felt intrinsic to the music and the storytelling, and even if her life had changed dramatically, ours hadn't, which meant that she was still reflecting them. Still, the tension between Swift as every girl and her mounting fame and fortune was growing. And then the VMAs happened.

She arrived in a horse-drawn carriage wearing a ball gown and a tiara. If you'd been a grade-school outcast, then channeled those youthful insecurities into the music that eventually turned into a platinum album and success beyond your wildest dreams you might be a little extra about it, too, but admittedly it was a little much. You almost certainly know the beats of what came next: Swift won the award for Best Female Music Video for "You Belong with Me" and got up to give her acceptance speech. "Thank you so much! I always dreamed about what it would be like to maybe win one of these someday, but I never thought it actually would have happened. I sing country music. So thank you so much for giving me the chance to win a VMA award! I—"

Suddenly, Kanye West, who'd walked the red carpet holding a bottle of Hennessy, was onstage with her. "Yo, Taylor, I'm really happy for you. And I'mma let you finish . . . But Beyoncé had one of the best videos of all time! One of the best videos of all time!"

I can visualize this whole scene. The camera panning to Beyoncé, staring horrified at the stage as she mouthed, "Oh, Kanye!" Swift, her five-eleven frame hunched over, clutching her Moon Man, frozen after awkwardly taking the microphone back from West. Many in the crowd booed, until MTV cut to a prerecorded segment between Eminem and Tracy Morgan.

According to a *Billboard* oral history, everything that night was every bit as much of a clusterfuck as it seemed. West went back to his seat and right after he did, Pink ran over to give him an earful. Both Swift and Beyoncé wound up crying backstage. Swift was scheduled to perform "You Belong with Me" during the following segment, and composed herself in time to do it, though you can hear in her voice that she's shaken. Van Toffler, the acting producer backstage who had the unenviable task of settling everyone down, hinted to Beyoncé that she was going to have some stage time to herself in not very long, and that it might be nice if she got Swift back up there. Swift and her mom only stayed after her performance because of pleas from Toffler. "There was a lot of begging," he said. At the end of the night, Beyoncé took home the top prize, which was well-deserved for "Single Ladies." She brought Swift back onstage to finish her speech during her time.

That night, West attempted to blog through it: "I'M SOOOOO SORRY TO TAYLOR SWIFT AND HER FANS AND HER MOM," he wrote. "I LIKE THE LYRICS ABOUT BEING A CHEERLEADER AND SHE'S IN THE BLEACHERS." Sort of! Whether intentionally or not, he'd tapped into the part of Swift's persona the public was growing skeptical about—that she was really as wide-eyed or vulnerable as the person in her songs. Initially, Swift did get the bulk of the sympathy. A video leaked of President Obama on a hot mic calling Kanye a "jackass." Kelly Clarkson asked if West had been hugged enough as a child on her blog (everyone had a blog). Katy Perry Tweeted in all caps: "FUCK U KANYE. IT'S LIKE U STEPPED ON A KITTEN." (Celebrities used to post like that!) But gradually, public opinion shifted in West's direction. Maybe it was that Swift's team seemed a little too eager to capitalize on the press. "The Kanye incident brought attention to Taylor, to an audience that did not really know her or her music," Borchetta told the *Wall Street Journal* in 2010. "And when they did check it out, they discovered that they really liked it." Maybe it was an acknowledgment of the racial politics of how an "angry Black man" interrupting an "innocent white girl" were being received. Maybe it was just that Swift seemed to keep winning, and people didn't like it. At the VMAs the following year, Swift performed a song from her third album, *Speak Now*, called "Innocent," which she wrote for West. It is earnest and forgiving to the point of being downright condescending, which critics pointed out. It became more and more popular for the media to argue that Swift was inauthentic or that she was treated with kid gloves, and even some genuine vitriol snuck in. Shortly after the 2010 VMAs, the website *Deadspin* published an article called "The Hater's Guide To Taylor Swift," which included a wish for Swift to wind up "blowing local Tennessee DJs in lieu of record company payola handouts." In 2012, *Salon* more tamely asked, "Is Taylor Swift Being Taken Too Seriously?" in a piece that came to the conclusion that she represented Americans' lowered expectations from life coming on the heels of the 2008 recession. Some of those arguments were in better faith than others, but the central question boiled down to wondering how it was possible that so many people cared so much about this one woman they didn't know.

That wondering was pretty loud online, as was the response to it. One reason the VMAs were such a big deal was that, well, everyone just wouldn't stop yapping about them. The 2009 VMAs were a major event in the development of Twitter—"Taylor, I'mma let you finish" became one of the first big pop-cultural events where people reacted immediately on social media, arguing and memeing in real time. Over a decade later, no artist and their fans have had a greater impact on the modes of fandom, and how stars interact with their supporters, than Swift and the Swifties, and that night was a turning point. Swift helped create many of our current online dynamics, particularly by helping shape internet culture around fandoms and affinities and fostering deep connections between those who share them. That started with how she built support and got her songs on the radio using social media at the outset of her career, but it certainly continued around events like the VMAs that created the kind of social chatter that helps fans find each other.

The point here is not to relitigate the VMAs, though I do think it's worth noting how long of a tail that event has had in both artists' careers, especially Swift's. A decade after she was interrupted onstage, events stemming from that incident were still actively shaping Swift's career and persona—her 2017 album, *Reputation*, was created during a retreat from the public eye after her 2016 "cancellation" stemming from Kim Kardashian's edited video of a seemingly friendly conversation with Kanye West about the song "Famous" that cast her as a liar and a villain, personas Swift played with on the album. (In 2017, the Twitter user Caitlin Bitzegaio summed this up well, posting: "When Kanye took that VMA from Taylor I was like 'oh weird,' not 'this will psychologically cripple both artists, driving them to madness.'") What I think is actually important, though, and perhaps the root of some of those lasting consequences, is how the show revealed the intensity of the relationships fans had formed with Swift, how many outsiders struggled to understand that, and how fans online banded together even more closely as a result.

By 2009, some friction between Swift's rapid ascension and underdog narrative was inevitable and maybe even necessary. Swift *is* a fighter: You can plot the chapters of her career by the various foils she's set her sights on vanquishing. Over time, for the most part, I think she's chosen them well—she's taken on Nashville's hardened misogyny, men who took advantage of her, her own reputation and the costs of fame, and, most recently, practices in the music industry itself through her Taylor's Version rerecording projects. But I don't think it's a coincidence that the most challenging moments of her career have come when her foils have been the least clear or least compelling. Swift's career began as a precocious young woman's quest to take on a country music world that didn't believe it had space for her, and watching her prove those assumptions wrong was both satisfying and made for great music—"Mean," the twangy, banjo-driven takedown of a critic who made fun of her voice is, to this day, one of her best songs. But as she began crossing over to pop, the foil was less obvious—she was always a good fit for pop because of who her core audience was, and pop radio had coveted her songs even when they *were* country songs. If she was a fighter, no one was fighting back, leaving her critics feeling like she was claiming to have taken hits that weren't really there. And wondering why a rich, white, beautiful woman, whose work was custom-fit to be celebrated by her chosen industry, was singing about how badly she'd been treated.

This is where the disconnect lies. For as much as I know how successful she was at this time, I did not feel like she was met with broad approval. Though I was a huge Taylor Swift fan in 2009, I also rarely would have described myself that way to others unless I was *sure* I was with people who agreed. Listening to Taylor Swift was a fairly private experience for me at least through a few years after the VMAs incident. My dominant high school memory of playing her music is going on long runs by myself to listen to *Speak Now*. How much of this was my insecurity about revealing my own tastes, particularly those that aligned with music I assumed was considered trivial, uncool, or too girly to be taken seriously? Probably a lot! But that was a pretty powerful feeling that, during the time it shaped my perspective on Swift, lent a lot of credence to her own underdog narrative. It seemed authentic because I related to it. That narrative wasn't just hers, it was mine, so of course I believed in it! When, during my sophomore year, an upperclassman boy got back together with his girlfriend after an extended flirtation with a friend of mine, something she quietly accepted even though she felt burned and used, I texted her the song "I Almost Do," off *Red*, which is about wanting to tell someone how you feel but holding back. It was the best way I had to tell her I got what she was experiencing.

When I think about the story of Swift in the first decade of her career, I think of two things: her rise in country and initial crossover to pop, and the development of her fan base, in concert with the rise of social media, into a hugely powerful tool. That started in 2006, when she turned her Myspace into a fan database and radio lobbying enterprise, and by the end of the 2000s the VMAs had revealed just how much passion and internet chatter she was capable of generating. She hasn't slowed since—no fan base today is bigger, more mobilized, or more aspirational for other artists, many of whom emulate Swift's online behavior, which fundamentally works to scale a type of intimacy with fans through social media. She's lurked so much on Twitter, Tumblr, and TikTok, popping up to like or comment on the occasional fan post, that the practice got its own name—TayLurking. Swift has always worked a lot of opportunities for her to point out at the audience—at some one fan—into her choreography, and TayLurking has a similar effect, communicating to her entire fan base that she does see them as individuals.

For example, in 2014, a Tumblr post went viral. Below a black-and-white picture of a smiling young blond girl wearing a tiara, the post read:

> This is a picture of my friend Becky. She used to be a happy, popular girl until one night she snorted marijuana at a party. She died instantly. Please, don't do marijuana. It's the most dangerous drug out there. Please don't wind up like Becky.

The user bitch-pudding reblogged the picture with a comment:

> pretty sure that's Taylor Swift

Crucially, the photo was very obviously of Taylor Swift. But a third commenter responded:

> no it's becky

For a while, this was just a moment of dumb Tumblr behavior. But that fall, Swift stepped out in New York City wearing a plaid skirt and a yellow shirt with the words "no it's becky" on the chest in the Tumblr font. Photos of her in the shirt instantly went viral, and "no it's becky" has remained a Swiftie in-joke ever since. It was a genuinely funny thing to do on her part, and especially savvy since it communicated to her fans that she was paying attention on a granular level. A hallmark of Swift's best music is specificity—stories told in such vivid detail that a listener feels like they've been in a room with her. She backs that feeling up in how she interacts with fans, whether the room is a stadium or, even more often, a chat room or a feed. In her choreography, she points at individuals in a crowd. During the Eras Tour, she placed the "22" hat on a different child's head every night. She'll notice if someone in the crowd gets engaged, or even if someone looks like they could use some help from stadium staff. The implication isn't that she'll interact with everyone, but that she *could* interact with anyone.

But as online life has become more and more synonymous with real life, fandoms like Swift's have become bigger and more visible features of the modern web, showcasing the public-private nature of the internet, where individuals, often under the guise of anonymity, routinely share their intimate thoughts in front of the entire world. Together, these individuals are a highly mobilized collective, and the pop stars that command these groups are highly sought after as political endorsements, salespeople, and bellwethers of public opinion. Swift is a beautiful songwriter, but the greatest narrative she's shaped is that of her career. As that's made her the biggest star on the planet, the importance of narrative has grown for pop stars in general and become the thing that mobilizes their audiences. Swift and the Swifties built modern fandom to be massive, persistent, and motivated—ignore them at your own peril.

9

When Rihanna
Met Reverb

PRO TOOLS WAS GLITCHING AGAIN. ANY VERSION OF THE
sound editing software tended toward bugginess in 2007, and let's
just say that the version Kuk Harrell and Tricky Stewart were working on wasn't quite top-of-the-line. The producer cousins had
worked on a handful of hits as individuals (Stewart, especially, had
a hand in some big R&B songs in the late nineties like Mýa's "Case
of the Ex," and had cowritten and produced the single "Me Against
the Music" for Britney Spears in 2003) and done some big commercial jingles as a team. But their production company was off to
a slow start. Since 2004, Harrell, Stewart, and their third partner,
The-Dream (hyphen his, I'm not sure why), had been working together at RedZone Entertainment, the production shop Stewart
had founded in Atlanta with help from the record executive L.A.
Reid. But it had been three years since Harrell joined on and the
"hitmaking" shop hadn't made any major hits, so they weren't caus-
ing a stink about having the absolute best in equipment.

The song they were working on was built off a prerecorded drum loop, a free preset from the recording software GarageBand. The hi-hats sounded tinny and a little cheap, but there was something about it that pulled Stewart into the room when he heard Harrell messing around with it. He added chords on a keyboard and a baseline using the programming software. The-Dream heard that and soon all three men were in the studio riffing together, trying to turn the track into a song. It had a four-beat cadence, and for some reason, the word "umbrella," stretched out into um-ba-rell-a so that it would fit four syllables, came into The-Dream's head. He went into the vocal booth and got on the mic, and words became phrases and phrases became a promise to a friend to protect them from the elements—that when it's raining more than ever, you'll still have each other. By this point, the RedZone crew had basically a whole demo, but they had also been running Pro Tools for a couple hours. They knew from experience that the name of the game was to finish recording before the program crashed, and that they probably didn't have long. The reverb plug-in, especially, had a reputation for glitchiness, so though they wanted to use it, they chose a workaround. Still in the vocal booth, The-Dream sang his own echoes: *ella, ella, ella, eh, eh, eh* . . . Good enough for a demo, they figured.

Harrell, Stewart, and The-Dream didn't know they had a *hit* hit, but they thought they'd put in a good day's work, and they wanted to get "Umbrella" to someone big. They tried Spears's team first but got shot down so quickly they weren't even sure if Spears herself ever heard the demo. Musically, "Umbrella" wouldn't have been at all out of place on *Blackout,* Spears's 2007 album that was her first record-length foray into electronic dance songs, but her label told the RedZone guys that she already had enough material. Their issue was likely more thematic—*Blackout* was recorded and released during one of the worst and most chaotic stretches of her life, in which her ability to parent her children was made a public spectacle, so having her sing about being a protector might have felt odd, or just depressing. More literally, if you googled "Britney Spears umbrella" that year, most of the results showed video of an incident at a gas station in which Spears attacked a paparazzo—one of many swarming her and her kids while she tried to fuel up her car—with an umbrella. It's not clear if this happened before or after Spears's team heard the "Umbrella" demo, but you can see how it could have been a deterrent. Britney just wasn't really in a place to say *It's okay, don't be alarmed.*

If not Britney, then who? Stewart sent the "Umbrella" demo around, including to Reid, who heard its potential. The only catch was that Reid wanted the song for an up-and-coming artist of his while Stewart wanted it to go to someone established. He said no at first, but Reid kept coming back. He had Jay-Z make a call. He offered more money. He wouldn't go away. Eventually, Stewart relented, and Harrell flew with the demo to Los Angeles to meet Robyn Rihanna Fenty for some studio time. Reluctant as the Red-Zone team might have been, it took just a few lines for Harrell to hear that she was all they'd need and more. Who needs reverb when you have RiRi?

The weakest part of "Umbrella" is the lyrics, a lot of which don't make sense. There's a whole part about how in the dark you can't see shiny cars, which is kind of strange. Another describes someone as part of the narrator's entity, there for infinity. It's all pretty clunky. But when Rihanna sings "Umbrella," the lyrics don't really matter. The most memorable lines are just syllables—the "eh-eh-ehs," and the way she pronounces "um-ba-rell-a." The meaning isn't the point. The point of "Umbrella" is that it's cool to listen to Rihanna say stuff.

Rihanna would go on to be one of the most prolific hitmakers ever and a defining artist of the late-aughts era in which electronic music merged with pop. "Umbrella" was her second number-one hit, but it was the song that set her on that course. She championed the EDM and dance-pop boom during a time when it was still finding its audience, and her preternatural cool and sense of presence ended up being the perfect counterweight to music that utilized key technological advancements. As this music became hugely popular, its fast dance-floor beats brought pure pop back to the center of popular music. And as computer technology was integral to this music, it provided a counterargument to the idea that there is anything wrong with "manufacturing" a pop song.

Before "Umbrella," Rihanna's biggest hits had been dancehall-inflected pop songs like "Pon de Replay" and "Break It Off." These songs nodded to her childhood in Barbados, where she started singing when she and some of her schoolmates decided to form a girl group called Contrast. When Rihanna was fifteen, she and Contrast got the chance to audition for a pair of American songwriters and producers, Carl Sturken and Evan Rogers, two guys who'd mostly written songs for *NSYNC, Christina Aguilera, and their lot but were both married to women from Barbados and therefore spent time there. They zeroed in on Rihanna, who they thought already had a star quality, and brought her to Connecticut to cut some early demos and take auditions. Her level of self-assuredness had not quite yet reached the leaving-Giorgio-Baldi-on-a-Tuesday-holding-a-full-glass-of-wine plane it has today—she bungled an early audition with Clive Davis and was terrified to meet Jay-Z when she went to Def Jam—but had a quality that came through in the latter meeting. Jay-Z wouldn't let her leave the building before the paperwork for her Def Jam deal was signed.

Rihanna's first album, *Music of the Sun,* is an obvious nod to her Caribbean roots. That's the album "Pon de Replay" comes from, and it's great. For the first single of her second album, though, there was some question over how far she should depart from dancehall. The song "SOS" had been offered to Christina Milian, who'd turned it down saying it was too poppy for her, and some of the people managing Rihanna at Def Jam wondered if she should have the same concern, whether the song was "Black enough" for her to sing. There's a great quote in John Seabrook's book *The Song Machine* that got everyone to stop worrying about this, though, which was L.A. Reid's response: "She's Madonna. She's an international pop star. Let's make the people dance." This became the Rihanna mission statement, and "Umbrella" was the song that synthesized that mission, even if it's less of a dance song than a song that uses a lot of the trappings of dance music.

Make the people dance was a strategy that worked. "Umbrella" was the first single from Rihanna's third studio album, *Good Girl Gone Bad,* and it lived at number one on the Hot 100 for seven weeks in the summer of 2007. This happened to coincide with a particularly wet stretch of weather worldwide. In Ireland, it rained for forty-nine days in a row, which is a lot, even for Ireland, where it was considered the wettest summer in a decade. Halfway across the world, New Zealand experienced flooding and tornadoes. Romania—Romania!—which had been experiencing drought conditions, was suddenly flooded with torrential rainfall. And so naturally, people thought about Rihanna, her side bangs, and her *um-ba-rell-a.* The coincidence became enough of a novelty news story that Rihanna herself was asked about why it was *raining, raining* quite so much. "I feel bad about that," she told the UK wire service World Entertainment News Network. "I don't think it's my fault. I think the weather helped to keep the song there for so long. It worked for me."

I'm unconvinced that Romanian flash flooding has a major impact on the *Billboard* charts, but yes, everything was coming up Rihanna. "Umbrella" quickly became the song of that summer and the biggest of her career up to that point. Its success established her musical signature: translating a building wave of dance music into massive hits, with her ineffable presence at the center.

By the time *Good Girl Gone Bad* arrived in 2007, new technologies were rapidly changing the sound of pop music. Some of those, like the GarageBand presets that became the baseline, were used directly in the making of the song. Another emerging tool was Auto-Tune, the digital audio workstation software that can pitch correct a singer's voice to the point of distortion. Auto-Tune had been around for over a decade—shout-out to Cher!—but it was becoming a more regular feature of mainstream pop music. Daft Punk, the French house duo, were trendsetters in their use of the tool, and their *Alive 2007* tour seeded a substantial amount of Americans' growing interest in both dance music and festival culture. That tour came on the heels of their Coachella set in 2006, their first show in the United States since 1997, a show they were able to take on the road effectively because of advancements in computers and lighting design that could support their spectacle of dazzling lights and electro euphoria. Sets like theirs contributed to the growing belief that pressing buttons on machines could be its own art form—in the audience of the show that day was a young Skrillex, who right then and there decided he wanted to be a DJ.

In the music world, new technologies have not always been met with open arms. It was a big deal in the sixties for Bob Dylan to plug in his guitar. In the eighties, the rock band Queen posted labels on several of their albums, proudly proclaiming "No Synthesizers!" Rage Against the Machine did the same in the nineties, though I guess you kind of have to figure on that one. After T-Pain started using Auto-Tune in 2005, subsequently sending twenty-seven sex-and-party jams up the Hot 100, he, too, faced backlash. If you've ever seen that man's Tiny Desk concert you know he can really sing, but in the Netflix documentary series *This Is Pop,* T-Pain talks about meeting Usher on a plane, only to have Usher tell him that he "fucked up music for real singers."

Artists in all genres navigate these stigmas. Queen eventually started using a *lot* of synthesizers, and I think people eventually came around on Dylan going electric. But the impulse to look down on music made with the help of machines is especially tough for pop music, since pop tends to struggle against the idea that it is "fake" or "manufactured." The anti-synth backlash in the eighties was really the rock establishment's backlash to disco, and the response to Auto-Tune not only reflects a rejection of technology, but also of pop, and especially dance music, where it found its first home. Generally, groups dead set on talking about "real" music tend to be at least a little skeptical of pop.

Dance music made with primarily electronic instruments—what we'd now call EDM or techno—rose up in the 1980s. Berlin was the European hub, but there were healthy scenes in the US in the Midwest, especially Detroit and Chicago. In the beginning, the techno boom was driven by groups of DJs who were excited to be on the cutting edge, with a range of synthesizers at their disposal and all-night club scenes eager to hear what they had to offer. But in the nineties, dance music fared better in Europe than in the United States. The rise of grunge, and its rejection of frothy disco, trivialized the genre. Many of the best American DJs moved to Germany or the United Kingdom. European tastes have a history of being less fickle when it comes to dance music, and I can't say I really understand what our deal is. There are whole sociocultural theories about how our lack of a class stratification system leads us to root our own elitist impulses in artistic taste. To be honest, that feels like a reach to me, but I also can't think of a better explanation for the fact that this country never really got behind Kylie Minogue, so maybe it holds.

But in the mid-2000s, the US was ready to welcome some euro dance back into our lives. Software like GarageBand and Auto-Tune fit well into this type of music, and producers were eager to use what was new and experimental. The canary in the coal mine was the song "Everytime We Touch" by the German group Cascada, which became a top-ten hit in 2006. Around this time, I recall playing "I Do, I Do, I Do" by the Danish group Creamy over and over on the *Dance Dance Revolution* machine at my local bowling alley, which had a similar vibe. Spears's *Blackout* was another harbinger. Party music was big in general, but a lot of the rap and R&B that had filled that role on the top spaces of the Hot 100 started to cede that territory to on-the-floor disco bangers. The rave-fairy aesthetic hadn't quite coalesced around EDM as a genre yet, but electronic dance music was slowly taking over. The EDM boom was one of the more literal results of the widened access to computer tools that spread throughout the 2000s—without those, Skrillex never wants to be a DJ, Kuk Harrell never finds the "Umbrella" beat on GarageBand, and no one uses Auto-Tune. But it needed a champion. And for the full stretch of that era, that was Rihanna.

"Umbrella" was the song where Rihanna got on the path to becoming the queen of dance-pop music, even though not every single on *Good Girl Gone Bad* was a dance number. The second, "Shut Up and Drive," is a rocker that samples New Order, and the third, "Hate That I Love You," is a sappy duet with Ne-Yo. But the two biggest—"Umbrella" and the fourth single, "Don't Stop the Music," were. This is who Rihanna was going to be. When *Good Girl Gone Bad* got a deluxe edition, one of the songs that showed up on it was

"Disturbia," another robo-club stomper. Rihanna was dating Chris Brown at the time, and they were musical collaborators as well. Brown had originally cowritten "Disturbia," thinking he'd record it himself. But he'd also signed a contract with Wrigley gum to write a new jingle for Doublemint, and that jingle became the song "Forever," which was a huge hit. Brown didn't want "Disturbia" to interrupt the momentum he had with "Forever," so he gave it to Rihanna. "Forever" got all the way to number two, but it never topped the Hot 100. Rihanna recorded "Disturbia" for the bonus edition of *Good Girl Gone Bad,* and, once again, people really liked hearing her sing syllables—*bam bam bi dum ba ba bi dum*—over a cool beat. The song jumped "Forever" and went to number one. She's Madonna. She's an international pop star. Just make the people dance.

By the end of 2007, Rihanna was one of the biggest stars on the planet, and her biggest hits were sounding more and more like dance music. For one thing, she was speeding up the tempo of the charts—if you listen to the Top 40 over the first few years Rihanna was releasing big songs, you can literally hear the pace of mainstream pop pick up. In 2020, the BBC did a study of the twenty bestselling songs (using UK chart data, which does vary somewhat from US numbers but shows similar trends) of the last twenty years and found that 2009 was the most up-tempo year during that period. In '09, the average hit galloped along at 124 beats per minute. This is an actual biological sweet spot: In their book *Switched On Pop,* the wonderful musicologists Nate Sloan and Charlie Harding point out that over the course of popular music history, the average tempo of Top 40 pop has hovered right around 120 beats per minute, what physiologists would call the human body's "preferred tempo." We like to walk at a rate of around 120 steps per minute, so 120 beats per minute creates a natural soundtrack. Dance music is not walking music, though, and a lot of Rihanna's big hits, which were part of this trend, clocked in even faster. "Disturbia" runs along at 125 beats per minute, the hook Rihanna sang on "Live Your Life," with the rapper T.I., clocked in at 160, and "Umbrella" was all the way up at 174.

Another way Rihanna embraced new technologies popular in dance music was through remixing. In 2009, she released an entire remix album of *Good Girl Gone Bad*, with a new club mix for each track. The remixes were all radio edits—formatted for airplay rather than just for the actual club—a tacit assumption that radio was a reasonable place to put something like the double-timed Moto Blanco mix of "Push Up On Me," which, increasingly, it was. The remix album got to number four on the Dance/Electronica chart.

A cousin of remixing existed in the form of mash-ups, another tech-based musical trend that was having a major moment and that Rihanna interacted with substantially. The "United States of Pop" mixes, a project by a young music engineer named Jordan Roseman, who went by the stage name DJ Earworm, had become a fixture in a San Francisco–based mash-up community and were a prime example. In 2007, Roseman decided it would be fun to try to mash up all twenty-five of the top *Billboard* songs of the year-one mix. The result was a tapestry of Fergie spelling out "Glamorous," Justin Timberlake's "What Goes Around . . . Comes Around," and Carrie Underwood snarling about that bleached-blond tramp in "Before He Cheats." Soulja Boy's "*YOOOOOO*." Maroon 5. Quite a bit of Akon. All the threads of crunk and *American Idol*–core and Warped Tour–adjacent flotsam and jetsam stitched together. And also Rihanna, since "Umbrella" was the year's defining single and where "United States of Pop 2007" got its baseline.

It was a novel way to listen back to the year, and the mash-up sounded better as a song in and of itself than it had any right to.

The '07 mix got enough traction for Roseman to do it again the next year. Rihanna was even more present on that mix—"Disturbia," "Whatever You Like," "Take a Bow," and "Please Don't Stop The Music" all factor into the 2008 version.

But 2009 was when "United States of Pop" really took off. That year, Roseman posted the mix to YouTube right before getting on a plane to Singapore. By the time he landed, it had gone viral. There were a million and a half views on YouTube. "United States of Pop" became the unofficial soundtrack of pregames and frat basements. If I am ever kidnapped and my captors ask me to lip-synch "United States of Pop 2009" for my freedom, I will be home by lunch.

Together, the mixes become a kind of meta-text on the emerging tools that were changing the way music was made and how it sounded—Roseman was using his innovations to reflect the charts, which were largely a reflection of the producers and artists who were pushing similar boundaries. In that sense, it's no wonder Rihanna was so heavily featured.

By 2009, Rihanna had five number ones. She was riding a major hot streak where her singles, or any track she jumped on as a feature, were basically automatic hits. But that year, her personal life took a dark turn when, the night before the Grammy Awards, Brown committed his assault. They were driving, she asked him about someone he was texting on the side, and he badly beat her for it, punching her in the face, biting her hands and fingers, and choking her in a headlock. She got away and the next day Brown turned himself in. He was charged with felony assault and making criminal threats, to which he pled guilty and was sentenced to five years of probation and six months of community service. Days after the attack, some of the Los Angeles cops who'd responded leaked photos of Rihanna's bloodied face to *TMZ*.

Rihanna did not want to become the public face of domestic

violence. She'd grown up in an abusive household and worked hard to get away from it, and she was furious that similar harm was threatening to define her life again after all she'd accomplished. She was ripping mad about the leaked photos; she hated seeing the images of herself over and over. She wanted to get back to work.

Her first single after the attack was a feature. On "Run This Town" with Jay-Z and Kanye West, she sings a big, soaring hook, and that song became a top-five hit. It came out just six months after the Grammys. Three months after that, *Rated R*, her fourth studio album, was released. The album didn't explicitly address Chris Brown or what had happened in Rihanna's life, but it was darker than anything she'd released up until that point. There are a lot of hard-rocking guitars on *Rated R*, on songs like "Rockstar 101" and "Russian Roulette," and there are a lot of metaphors about weaponry and rough sex. (I know in hindsight that seems like a complicated place to go after a domestic violence incident, but recall that this was the original *50 Shades of Grey* moment, and mainstream content about bondage was de rigueur.) But the song that popped off was the lightest on the album, the dancehall jam "Rude Boy." Which is about Rihanna asking a guy if his dick is big enough for them to have sex.

"Rude Boy" was both in and out of step with the moment. By this point, nearing the end of the decade, the dance movement Rihanna had helped start was in a frothy, ridiculous place. The artists who had picked up the mantle of putting their force of personality into euro-disco frames did so with silliness, camp, and abandon. Lady Gaga was dressing up as David Bowie, Kesha was brushing her teeth with Jack Daniels, and Katy Perry was squirting whipped cream out of her boobs. "Rude Boy" is not like this. First of all, Rihanna is completely serious in her delivery of the song. *Boy is you big enough* is not a rhetorical question. She's almost completely deadpan, save for a tiny wink. I find this funny in a way that's still cool, which, if you're going to make a big-tent pop song explicitly about fucking, is really the best way to do it. But "Rude Boy" was almost dumb in a way that was right for that moment. The American economy was tanking and there was enough going on that was serious, so no one wanted anything dour in their pop songs. Rihanna radiating supreme coolness while half hitting on, half openly mocking a guy she's about to lay it down with is a lot of things, but it's definitely not dour. Rihanna's label didn't think it would be a huge hit since it was out of step with the rest of the album, and it was only the fourth single. But people loved it. It became her sixth number-one hit, and it served a huge (no pun intended) purpose in helping Rihanna reestablish herself in a way she liked.

She was back on her roll. Her fifth album, *Loud,* sent three songs to number one and had another, "Cheers (Drink To That)," reach the top ten. She sang the hook on Kanye's "All of the Lights." She went bowling with Drake, who then featured on "What's My Name?," one of the chart-toppers from that album cycle, and spent the next several years telling interviewers how he was sad Rihanna didn't pay more attention to him, which only made her seem more like a baddie. Rihanna went on tour, and for the European leg, her opener was a British DJ whose dance beats were rising up the charts in the United Kingdom. His name was Calvin Harris.

While they toured together, Harris presented Rihanna with "We Found Love," the track that would wind up as the basis for the most galactically, skull-bustingly epic song of a galactically, skull-bustingly epic career. Most of Rihanna's early hits used the stylings of dance music, but they were structured as pop songs. They built to a chorus or a hook, not a thumping dance-floor drop. But "We Found Love" is an actual rave song. The climax is the gale-force bass drop, over which Rihanna doesn't sing. But when she is providing vocals, she floats. Somehow, Rihanna delivers the dance floor's euphoric bliss and aggressive pulse all in one. The combination of the track's sheer abandon and the charisma of her presence is magical. The song hit number one almost instantaneously. It stayed there for over two months. "We Found Love" is still the biggest hit of Rihanna's, or Harris's, career. It's a preposterously big song. And it's the culmination of the years Rihanna had spent by that point working more and more elements of electronic dance music up the mainstream pop charts. It made Harris a massive star in his own right, too, as one of the first DJs truly treated as a real artist by mainstream fans.

After "We Found Love," Rihanna kept making songs that were even more explicitly for the dance floor than her earlier work— "Where Have You Been," another single from *Talk That Talk,* the album that "We Found Love" was on, employs dubstep. In 2012, she released "Right Now" with the French DJ David Guetta. In 2016, she worked with Harris again, singing the vocal on "This Is What You Came For," a song ghostwritten by Harris's then girlfriend Taylor Swift, under the pen name Nils Sjöberg. (In Swift's "Look What You Made Me Do" music video, there's a graveyard with a tombstone engraved with that name.)

Rihanna didn't need EDM. She sounds great singing dancehall. She can do rock 'n' roll. One of my favorite of her songs, "Desperado," off 2016's *ANTI,* is a Western-inflected alt-R&B waltz, and she *crushes* it. But by embracing the tools of EDM, Rihanna attached herself to songs that were new and cutting-edge. And I do think that EDM needed Rihanna. She was the perfect vehicle for the genre because of her presence. Rihanna always sounds cool, but she never sounds *impersonal,* even when she's breaking through layers of electronica. She's the beating heart thumping at the center of the dance floor. Rihanna would become the dominant singer of this dance-pop era, and I think it's because of the qualities in her voice that make the most impersonal kind of club songs sound intimate or cheeky. (It's also just because Rihanna is really fucking cool.) When the *eh, eh, eh* lines on "Umbrella" run through this processor, they manage to keep their lilting Barbados texture. They get the futuristic Auto-Tune sound, but they still sound like they're coming from a person—this person. The kind of person who gets Drake all bent out of shape after hanging out twice, or the number-one person you care about seeing at the Met Gala. Dance music would have had a moment in the late aughts no matter what—music always finds a way to take advantage of the new tools it has available— but I do think there's a real chance that that moment could have been slightly more marginal without Rihanna. People just like her. They want to spend time doing whatever she's doing.

EDM, and even dance music in general, is just one segment of pop music. But because the *electronic* element means that it deals specifically with music made by machines, it's a style that pushes back against the notion that to consider a song "manufactured" is to invalidate it. Of course, this idea didn't completely go away. At the 2012 Grammys, accepting the Foo Fighters' award for Best Rock Performance, front man Dave Grohl talked about making music the old-fashioned way. "To me this award means a lot because it shows that the human element of music is what's important," Grohl said. "Singing into a microphone and learning to play an instrument and learning to do your craft, that's the most important thing for people to do. . . . It's not about being perfect, it's not about sounding absolutely correct, it's not about what goes on in a computer. It's about what goes on in here [your heart] and what goes on in here [your head]." The statement ruffled enough feathers that Grohl felt the need to log on and clear things up. "I don't know how to do what Skrillex does (though I fucking love it) but I do know that the reason he is so loved is because he sounds like Skrillex, and that's badass," he posted. "We have a different process and a different set of tools, but the 'craft' is equally as important." Grohl signed the post Davemau5.

In a time when technological experimentation in music was still met with a spattering of eye rolls and scoffs, Rihanna's success with pop dance and EDM helped usher in a wave of EDM in the states that became embraced as inventive, leading to other artists like Lady Gaga and Kesha, and DJs like Calvin Harris and David Guetta, to experiment musically in related ways. EDM peaked around the end of the 2000s, and a few years later it was no longer as major a fixture on the charts. But after electronic music had dominated as the true center of pop, it was harder to dismiss any music on the grounds that its creation was "manufactured" and aided by technology. A traditional musician like Dave Grohl might bark at the new, but the fact that he came around quickly with apologies to Skrillex further highlights that shift. As technology has been a bigger and greater feature of the cutting edge of pop, it has become harder to deny that there isn't an artistry to machines and people putting songs together, or to the ability to take electronic sounds and inject them with their own personality and humanity. Rihanna's career traced the emergence of these trends, and by the time she hit her peak, they were impossible to ignore.

10

Little Monsters Everywhere

MY FRESHMAN YEAR OF HIGH SCHOOL BEGAN IN THE FALL of 2008, and the first dance of the school year was always the Video Dance. As you can probably imagine, it was called that because it was held in a gym where a couple giant projector screens were hung from the rafters so that music videos could be played all over the walls. My couple-hundred-student middle school in rural Vermont had school dances, but they were small affairs, where you knew all the moms who chaperoned. My high school was one of the biggest prep schools in New England, and definitely a different scene. A few hours before the dance, the air wafting out of the bathrooms in my dorm was thick with clouds of Bath & Body Works glitter body spray and the mingling smells of Marc Jacobs Daisy and Clinique Happy. One of the girls in my hall introduced me to the concept of a Sugarlips tank top, those stretchy, ribbed feats of engineering designed to lift one's chest to roughly chin height, lent me one of hers, and suggested I switch from a middle part to a side part, which is to say she changed my life. We made a pact with the rest of the hall to walk over to the dance together a little while after it started. I coated my eyelashes with drugstore mascara, ironed my hair pin straight, and, I cringe to say, paired the tank top with a pair of Nike shorts rolled over twice at the waistband. I was as ready as I'd ever be. We scaled the steps up to the gym's entryway, and with doors wide open, were greeted with the image of several hundred of our sweaty new peers smooshed together—the ancient practice now known as grinding—in the glow of the two massive projector screens displaying the music video of the song of the moment, Lady Gaga's "Just Dance."

The "Just Dance" video features a platinum blond Gaga with thick bangs and a Bowie-esque lightning bolt sticker on her face crashing a house party that has seemingly already raged to conclusion, then starting it back up again. To a steady disco beat and tinny synthesizer chords, she stomps from room to room, restoring the party one ridiculous dance move at a time. She rides an inflatable orca in a kiddie pool. She spins a disco ball. She licks her finger while holding direct eye contact with the camera. It's a little burlesque, but she's not trying to be sexy. The part that Gaga is playing is wasted club rat. She wants you to know one thing, and it's that she is *so fucked up right now*.

Gaga has no idea where she is in "Just Dance." She doesn't know the name of the club, nor what is going on in it. She can't find her keys, her drink, or her man, and she's lost her phone. She's had a little bit too *much, much* of something, of what doesn't really matter. There is only one thing left to do.

Just dance / gonna be okay da da doo-doo-mmm

Yes, this was all going to be very different.

How to describe the vibes. . . . You know that John Mulaney

joke about how every song is about "how tonight is the night and we only have tonight"? He is referring to the years 2008 to 2012, I'm sure of it. These were the years of the convergence of Obama-era optimism and post-recession doom and gloom, when the dueling instincts to celebrate or to let loose from life's anxieties led to some cultural mass hedonism. These vibes were represented in music; as the influx of EDM quickened tempos and computer-generated sounds became de rigueur features of pop music, the stories and aesthetics pop stars told and played with became correspondingly rage-tastic. It felt as though there were two kinds of songs in those days: songs about what crazy shit had happened last night and songs about how crazy things were going to get *tonight*. We were going to rock this club and go all night. We all had a feeling that tonight was going to be a good night. Last Friday night, well, that was obviously wild, too—tabletops, too many shots, and all.

Like a party raging into the wee hours, the lasting impact of this era was that it allowed pop stars to let loose and be weird, which wound up being quite the boon, artistically. Led by Lady Gaga, the most influential pop star of this era, pop in general embraced its flamboyance, its roots in queer culture, and its interest in the art world. As artists like Katy Perry and Kesha followed in Gaga's footsteps, they did not always play as insightfully as she did with these flamboyant aesthetics, and often toed a fine line between empowerment and frattish sleaze. Those lesser moments inspire cringes in hindsight, but the lasting impact of this era is an image of pop stardom that's not just tied to conventional sex appeal, but to spectacle rooted in self-expression, transgression, and true artistry.

There's a musical argument for why this happened, which is that this music was a much-needed correction. Pop had gone through a couple of flop years in 2006 and 2007, just before the EDM boom, a time I remember for how much the radio sounded like the *One*

Tree Hill soundtrack all the time. Snow Patrol played every five minutes. In 2006, the biggest single of the year was Daniel Powter's "Bad Day," which got big as the walk-off music for contestants getting kicked off *American Idol. Idol* in general probably had an outsized influence on this period—the show had had its moments with Kelly Clarkson and Carrie Underwood and Jordin Sparks, especially, but there was a fair amount of unnecessary crooning going on as well. (In 2006, thirty million people tuned in each week to watch Taylor Hicks.) This music had its purpose—to soundtrack TV scenes in which handsome doctors perished tragically—but it could also get deeply, deeply annoying. To this day, the sound of James Blunt makes me viscerally angry. To be clear, I'm speaking from the perspective of an eighth grader, a prisoner of Top 40 radio during a time when playlisting made stations homogenized enough that the whiny soft-rock balladry I'm talking about felt genuinely inescapable.

The primary form of popular music that reflected the hedonism of recession-era pop culture was, initially, southern crunk. Crunk originated in Memphis clubs in the nineties and migrated to Atlanta, where rappers like Lil Jon and groups like Three 6 Mafia were making aggressive party music. On its face, crunk is a subgenre that has no place on mainstream pop radio. These songs were feral bangers from the strip club performed by absurd men who were always screaming at you through their gilded teeth. Even the titles always seemed to be shouting: "Get Buck In Here," "Get Low," "Snap Yo Fingers." The lyrics tended to be downright filthy. "Get Low" had to have three separate radio edits (*'til the sweat drop down and fall*) owing in part to the fact that it took the radio folks a minute to figure out what "skeet" meant. Ludacris, during this period, had a persistent habit of bringing up people's mothers. Some of these songs were just too good to deny and got played anyway, and some others tried to be smart and toe the line. "Yeah!" by Usher featuring Lil Jon and Ludacris had the reckless energy of crunk but was also attached to Usher's pop-R&B mix. And while it's not exactly clean, there's no cursing. "Yeah!" got to number one on the Hot 100, representing crunk's mainstream apex, and we all shouted the *lady on the street but a freak in the bed* parts at school dances. Skeet skeet gotdamn, indeed.

Crunk met the moment, but it was an awkward fit on mainstream radio. But there just hadn't been much pure pop coming out that matched its energy. You were not going to catch Daniel Powter singing *lean over to the front and touch yo toes,* and that was the point. It was all just a little boring. Enter: Stefani Germanotta, stage right, wearing an elaborate headpiece.

Née Stefani Joanne Angelina Germanotta, Lady Gaga grew up in New York City on the Upper West Side. She went to private school and was a classmate of Nicky Hilton. (Nicky Hilton, who along with Paris randomly lived with Kesha and her mom for an episode of *The Simple Life,* is some kind of reverse grim reaper for the authors of the late-2000s high-camp electro-pop boom.) Gaga was a theater kid, obviously, and wound up at NYU Tisch where she wrote a thesis on Spencer Tunick, the photographer who documents crowds of naked people. She started a band and made the rounds in clubs on the Lower East Side like the Bitter End with other New York electro-freaks. She was having a hard time getting a record deal. When Def Jam signed her in the fall of 2006, Gaga wrote a poem on her website that referred to the pairing as a "white wedding." It was wacky—Gaga rhymed "jet black veil" with "no longer for sale," and made a vow to rock hard and be retro.

It is . . . a lot to unpack, but I think it's proof that behind the meat dresses and all the hoopla, Gaga is secretly one of our most earnest pop stars. A few months after she wrote that, Def Jam dropped her and she was devastated. She did get a songwriting deal, though, and got a few credits on songs like "Quicksand," a bonus track on Britney Spears's *Circus* album, and "Full Service," a deep cut on New Kids on the Block's reunion album *The Block*. And most importantly, she met Akon, who finally understood what she was all about.

He signed her to his label, the Interscope imprint KonLive, and paired her with RedOne, a Moroccan producer who'd done several years apprenticing in the Swedish studios of Max Martin disciples. Gaga and RedOne really liked each other. They did bits. In one of their first sessions at his studio in Queens, they joked around about what a feminized Mötley Crüe would sound like, a concept that became the song "Boys Boys Boys." But also an idea that ended up running through Lady Gaga's debut album *The Fame,* which was taking the structures of rock songs but executing them entirely with electronic production, like the synth riff that opens up "Just Dance."

Gaga and RedOne wrote "Just Dance" and "Poker Face" together within their first week working together. Akon was thrilled. He wanted to take the songs to Interscope boss Jimmy Iovine himself, because he worried that label politicking could mess with a good thing. His instincts were right: Iovine initially asked if Gaga and RedOne could give the songs to the Pussycat Dolls, which is a weird *Sliding Doors* moment. He was also worried that Gaga had too much in common with Gwen Stefani. But Akon insisted. He believed in Gaga and in the collection of songs she and RedOne had going, especially "Just Dance." To give the song a boost he figured he'd feature on the track, but wound up getting blocked by his label, since weirdly enough Akon wasn't signed to his own imprint. He was with Universal, Interscope's parent company, but there was enough competition and internal tension between the two parts of the organization that Universal said no, which is why "Just Dance" includes a verse by a full-on rando named Colby O'Donis who was never seen or heard from again. In hindsight, there was a perfect opening for Gaga. There was no way the James Blunts could keep ruling radio forever. (James Blunt has a ski chalet in Verbier, Switzerland, so I can make fun of him as much as I want.) Dance music wound up filling much of this void. EDM was creeping its way onto the radio through pop songs like Britney Spears's "Womanizer," Rihanna's "Disturbia," and Justin Timberlake's "SexyBack," as well as T-Pain's auto-tune. Gaga wasn't exactly making EDM tracks, but some of that DNA was coiled up in her from the days when she'd perform to electronic beats at clubs with just a keyboard and a laptop. In the moment, though, no one other than Akon was looking for someone doing what Lady Gaga was doing. That's probably because you couldn't dream up the idea of Lady Gaga if you tried, and it also explains why she had to hustle as hard as she did.

"Just Dance" came out in April 2008, and it was a hit in Europe almost immediately. But American radio didn't get it. Too weird. Bring on more Snow Patrol. The song would eventually climb to number one in January 2009, but the twenty-two weeks it took to get there marked the slowest climb for a song to the top spot since 2000, when Creed took twenty-seven weeks for "With Arms Wide Open" to peak. What happened during those twenty-two weeks was that Gaga hit the pavement. Interscope plastered posters of her face on plywood all around New York City. They handed out free copies of *The Fame* at car dealerships. When the song caught on somewhere, in Canada or in the gay clubs of San Francisco, Gaga would get on a plane and make an appearance or do a performance. She said yes to every TV show that would have her: Between 2008 and 2009 Gaga performed on *So You Think You Can Dance, The*

Ellen DeGeneres Show, The Tonight Show with Jay Leno, Good Day New York, The View, at the 57th Miss Universe pageant, the 2008 NewNowNext Awards (I don't know), and *American Idol.* The *Idol* performance is especially fun to revisit. Gaga sings "Poker Face," and she starts the song sitting at a pink piano filled with bubbles and plastic starfish with a man playing the violin standing next to her. She sings the first chorus and verse at the piano in a style that's half Bette Midler, half Amy Winehouse. She ends that first section with a little trill on the piano, then suddenly, the recorded beat of the song starts blaring from the speaker system. Gaga stands from the piano in a black-and-silver leotard with a big star cutout on one shoulder, and dancers in black suits rush onto the stage to form a wall behind her, moving in coordinated, robotic movements for the rest of the number. Just before it ends, Gaga goes on this frantic alien-disco dance break while the violinist absolutely wails on his instrument, and then the music drops out and she stares directly to camera. She is so fucking serious about this, and you can tell. At the time, Gaga was a few months away from meeting fashion creative Nicola Formichetti on a magazine shoot (who she would quickly bond with and add to her team as a creative director and conspirator on outfits, music videos, and other visuals), but in the moment she was the mastermind behind her image.

The best part of the performance is that right after Gaga finishes, the camera pans to the judges, who are standing and cheering, and then to the contestants, who are completely dumbstruck by the realization that if this is what it takes, they do not have it.

Early Gaga was doing a lot of stuff that subverted the male gaze pop stardom traditionally appealed to. She was also representing queer culture in mainstream art in a way that was unusually blatant, and therefore unusually meaningful. Gaga is a student of the game, and she knows when she's referencing Bowie and Madonna and Fosse and why she's referencing it. That's all really rad, obviously, but I can't claim I was that clued in to the significance of how she presented herself around those first singles. What I do remember being compelled by was the fact that you just had no idea what she was going to do next. She had fake blood start spewing from her rib cage during a performance of "Paparazzi" at the VMAs that ended with a lifeless, bloody Gaga hanging from the rafters. This was at the 2009 VMAs, and right after Beyoncé brings Taylor Swift onstage at the end of the show to make amends for Kanye, the camera pans over to Gaga in the crowd, covered in white face paint and wearing some kind of wreath around her face. In the "Telephone" video, she conspired with Beyoncé to murder Tyrese, a project that marked the beginnings of Beyoncé's own forays into more outlandish and transgressive work. Gaga, along with Rihanna and Britney Spears, was at the beginning of the major dance-pop trend that defined the last few years of the 2000s and the first few years of the 2010s, and she's a significant figure in that arc. But the legacy that's Gaga's first and foremost isn't musical, it's in her persona, as the most notable star of her era to make *weirdness* a fundamental part of her identity. Lady Gaga massively expanded the Overton window for how pop stars could look, dress, and act. And a big part of that was making it seem cool to act like a complete freak.

Once Gaga set the mold, other pop stars followed, playing with outlandish aesthetics. A primary example is Katy Perry. In 2005, while Gaga was working in New York trying to get traction with a label, Perry was a young singer-songwriter with a Christian rock background spending a lot of time in Los Angeles music venues trying to connect with people in the industry. One person she got to know was Butch Walker, the rocker and producer who'd had a major hand in Avril Lavigne's second album, *Under My Skin*. They met one evening after a show at the Hotel Cafe, where a lot of music types tended to showcase themselves.

"She had the art of the hustle down," Walker told me. "She was definitely the mover and the shaker, you could tell. I remember, she stopped me in the hallway and she's like, 'Butch Walker! We've got to work together, I would love to work together sometime.'"

They did get together, with Walker producing on tracks as Katy wrote. She was obsessed with Alanis Morissette and was playing with that kind of vibe in the pop-punk lane, so they worked on guitar-heavy songs. Their sessions produced a handful of tracks, including two that wound up on her debut *One of the Boys*—the pop-rock-inflected title track and the ballad "Thinking of You." At the time, the album was called *Fingerprints*. Beyond the songs she wrote with Walker, Perry was working with other heavyweights like Max Martin and Dr. Luke at a time when they were at their most engaged with the rockish sounds they were using with Kelly Clarkson and Pink. "I Do Not Hook Up," a song off Clarkson's third album, *All I Ever Wanted*, was originally written for Perry. But her label—she'd been signed to Columbia since 2005—sat on it. Walker wouldn't have known what was going on, but he was signed to Columbia imprint Epic Records at the time and happened to take a meeting about starting up his own vanity label there as a producer. He didn't end up taking the gig, but the label head who pitched the song offered up some interesting information, which was that they were considering dropping Perry.

"I was like, 'Uh, maybe go back and listen to it again because the guy you're sitting here courting and wanting to be part of the label as a staff producer and an imprint just produced two songs on that,'" Walker said, describing his response.

Perry did get dropped, but she and *Fingerprints* were immediately picked up by Rob Stevenson, the head of Capitol Records at the time.

"And the rest is platinum history," Walker said.

The album delay was probably a blessing in disguise for Perry. When she was hanging out with Walker, he'd taken her to see the Sounds, a Swedish indie rock band playing at the Fonda Theatre. The Sounds did kind of an eighties Blondie thing, and Perry was really into it. "She was sitting there losing her mind over it and being like, 'Oh, this is what I want to sound like, I want it to sound like this, I want it to feel like this,'" Walker said. He knew what his two songs on the album sounded like, and he figured the rest was pretty much in line with that pop-rock style. But after the record had sat shelved for about a year, a new A&R guy at Capitol called him asking him to update the tracks to fit in better with dance-pop radio.

"That stuff we'd done for her record was pretty organic, like it was all bass, guitar, drums, keyboards. It was poppy and shiny, but it was all done with real instruments," Walker said. "It wasn't dance music, which is mostly synthetic instruments and beats, which at the time was starting to get really popular on pop radio, hence Katy wanting to switch gears and make it more like that, which was smart of her on her part. I think it was genius."

Between the original sessions and the *One of the Boys* release date, the dance boom had started and Perry wanted to get in on it. And she had the right vehicle for this on what was now called *One of the Boys*—the lead single "I Kissed a Girl." If you're getting that Katy Perry had a weird vibe with gender in her early days, you're on to something. Perry was raised in Santa Barbara by two Pentecostal ministers, and secular music had been forbidden in their house. In 2017, while accepting an award from an LGBTQ+ rights organization, she said that as a kid she was sent to "pray the gay away at

Jesus camp," though what actually ended up happening was she got really into Morissette. So to some degree, she probably earned that clumsy approach to describing the dynamics of sexuality honestly. Perry has obviously evolved in her politics and presentation since then and has gone on to have a significant queer fan base. But "I Kissed a Girl" was a little cringey, especially since Perry had released an early track called "Ur So Gay," which criticizes its subject for being *so gay and you don't even like boys.* "Ur So Gay" is icky and its also a bad song, and it shares some of the questionable identity politics of "I Kissed a Girl," which plays off the sleazy, *Girls Gone Wild*–era depiction of intimacy between women as pure titillation that only happens with the express purpose of getting guys really turned on. *I hope my boyfriend won't mind it,* Perry winks on the chorus.

"I Kissed a Girl," though, unlike "Ur So Gay," is a great song. It has a melody that builds and beckons, but that melody exists within a wall of hyper-polished glam rock that never lets up. No matter what volume you listen to "I Kissed a Girl" at, it always sounds loud. "I Kissed a Girl" is another Max Martin– and Dr. Luke–produced song, and it came at a transitional time in both of their careers. The song has a lot of the same drums and guitars you hear on the rock-inflected hits they'd done with Clarkson, but it was more of a party song. You don't really dance to "Since U Been Gone," but you can definitely dance to "I Kissed a Girl." That's what Perry did in the music video for the song, which is also kind of sleazy in a *Girls Gone Wild* kind of way, but fit within the *going-out* aesthetics of the era. You could easily have mistaken the video for a Brandy Melville ad. Perry doesn't kiss anyone, but she and a bunch of girls in lingerie dance around together at a slumber party. And if you look closely, you'll notice that one of those girls was Kesha.

Kesha was still a few months away from her big break singing the

auto-tuned refrain on Flo Rida's "Right Round," a song about looking at butts at a strip club. But within the year, she'd sing the ultimate Hot Mess anthem, a defining song of *we only have tonight*–era
songwriting, even though it technically takes place in the a.m.

Wake up in the morning feeling like P. Diddy.

Obviously, that line reads differently now, but in its time it was
instantly iconic. Who wouldn't want to know more? What were the
circumstances under which this lithe, freckled blond girl was feeling like a record exec before she'd even had her coffee? Was she also
considering developing a line of oversized athleisure and fur coats?

She went on—turns out, her average day consisted of hitting the
town with just her sunglasses and brushing her teeth with Jack
Daniels before going out all night. This experience objectively
sounds awful. It's terrible dental hygiene. There's no way this person is sleeping enough. She has her sunglasses, but she's not coming
back home before the evening, so she's going to have them on her
all night and that's probably going to get annoying and she may not
have room for them in her bag. And yet—this is all going well
enough that this woman feels like executive Sean Combs when she
gets up in the morning?

When "TiK ToK" came out, a lot was made about Kesha potentially representing the arrival of the white female rapper. But in a
New York Times piece about this idea, Kesha—then going by Ke$ha—
explained where she saw herself coming from, which had nothing
to do with rap: "I'm trying to go for the lost-member-of-Whitesnake
vibe." This was it exactly. Kesha was hard-partying and ridiculous,
and for people who were starting to say things like "YOLO!" and
use appropriated words like "ratchet," she was an aspirationally
trashy queen. This is such a funny era to think back on now. I am

approaching thirty, and the only things that are aspirational to me now are comfortable shoes and an ultra-moisturizing skincare routine. But these were the days when I coveted metallic lamé miniskirts from American Apparel I had absolutely no use for, the "going-out" top was an entire wardrobe category, and bandage dresses abounded. For Halloween 2011, my high school friends and I dressed up in tight cotton American Apparel minidresses in bright primary colors and went to a school dance as *sexy Teletubbies*. Don't check, I have scrubbed all photographic evidence of this from the internet.

At the height of this Recession-pop era, this rowdiness and the actual boundary-pushing art that was happening simultaneously coexisted messily. The party girl aesthetic, especially, was a bit of a paradox because a lot of it was quite blatantly about appealing to men and displaying a comfort level with wild, unattached sexuality. But a lot of it was also grungy in a way that was a lot less prim and perfect than the ways artists like Britney Spears or Taylor Swift had been presented, which was considered freeing, both for consumers and pop stars. The catharsis matched the political and social moment, giving pop, always fighting accusations of being shallow, new depth. And because that catharsis hinged on expressiveness, pop stars got permission to be stranger, wilder, and more creative.

Kesha's persona is particularly complicated since she filed a lawsuit alleging she was raped by Dr. Luke, who produced "TiK ToK" and many of her other early hits and whose Kemosabe label Kesha was signed to, and lost several years of her peak to a strenuous legal battle that kept her away from making music. (Dr. Luke denied raping or ever having sex with Kesha and filed a countersuit against her for defamation. They eventually settled their dispute in June 2023 shortly before the case was to go to trial.) Kesha also described her working environment around this time as one in which she was pressured to live this kind of party-hardy lifestyle as well as perform it. But in the performance alone, there's also a kind of power: Kesha is totally comfortable being a ridiculous freaky weirdo who's only into guys that look like Mick Jagger and doesn't take any shit about it.

Kesha kept the glittery rave-girl thing going for a while. Her first album, *Animal,* had four top-ten hits on it, including "TiK ToK," which was a number-one hit. The follow-up single was "Blah Blah Blah," a sort of "TiK ToK" remake that featured sleazy Colorado electronic duo 3OH!3, who I have to admit had a pretty intense hold on me with the lines *so tell your boyfriend, if he says he's got beef / then I'm a vegetarian and I ain't fucking scared of him* from their 2009 single "Don't Trust Me," which made a nice run up the charts despite including the actual line *Do the Helen Keller and talk with your hips.* Kesha's two other singles that hit the top ten were "Your Love Is My Drug" and "Take It Off," a song she has said was inspired by a drag show, though not everybody necessarily got that. Dr. Luke built the "Take It Off" chorus off the classic "snake-charmer" melody, and you imagine they were going for an "exotic" feel for Kesha to sing about a place downtown where the freaks all come around.

It's hard to know what Kesha's career trajectory would have been like if she'd had a better partner in those early days. Her recent albums haven't been anywhere near as commercially successful, but I really enjoyed *Rainbow,* and songs like "Woman" and "Let 'Em Talk" have the same goofy exuberance without any of the baggage. That's not to say she's had another "TiK ToK," or that that song would work quite as well now despite how catchy it is. This era toed a line between sleaze and expressiveness, and sometimes it took some trial and error to figure out where the line really was. Katy Perry is probably the ultimate success story in doing that—with her second album, *Teenage Dream,* she managed to harness all the over-the-top iconography that worked on *One of the Boys,* with less of the weird subtext. This helped market one of the biggest pop albums ever; Perry wound up with a whopping five number-one hits off *Teenage Dream*—"California Gurls," the title track, "Firework," "E.T.," and another *how drunk were we last night* anthem in "Last Friday Night (T.G.I.F.)." For the *Teenage Dream* album cover, Perry wound up enlisting the artist Will Cotton to paint her. It was a chance collaboration—Perry was interested in buying one of Cotton's paintings, mostly pop art fantasy landscapes where all the features are made out of candy and sweets, sometimes with a pinup-style girl in their midst. When she emailed him, he wrote back asking if she would pose.

"I noticed she had this kind of pinup look," Cotton said. "And that was something I was looking for in the painting that I was making at the time."

Perry said yes, and that partnership became the *Teenage Dream* album cover, a pastel dreamscape of Perry lying naked on a cotton candy cloud that's billowing in all the right places.

It was perfect album art because *Teenage Dream* is pure sugar rush. The song "Teenage Dream" loosely describes the act of losing one's virginity, but what it really communicates is the moments of young exuberance that make you feel like the entire world is open wide in front of you, even when you're actually doing something kind of dumb and basic. It's the song equivalent of vanilla vodka and Coke in a red Solo cup: It's only perfect because you don't know any better, but that doesn't matter. This was Perry's second single in a row that basked in a forever-young kind of fantasy: On "California Gurls," Perry and featured artist Snoop Dogg greeted their loved ones and asked us to take a journey to the golden coast, land full of daisy dukes with bikinis on top. These singles both went to number one, and this fantasy helped Perry match Michael Jackson's *Thriller* as just the second album to get five separate hits to the top spot on the Hot 100. All five were constructed by the team of Martin, Dr. Luke, and Benny Blanco, and it's complicated to think about those men (mostly Luke) being so closely involved in crafting the fantasy. But it didn't come out as something made for men to ogle. The fantasy of "Teenage Dream" is in its nostalgia, and "California Gurls" might be so hot they'll melt your popsicle, but the dream of the song is to be one, not to have one. Even when Perry was shooting whipped cream out of her bra, the intent wasn't to be sexy. It was just about having fun, which during this time marked equally by joy and anxiety is all we were looking for.

After posing for the album cover, Katy called Cotton back to ask if he'd help out with the "California Gurls" music video, which was to be another Candyland extravaganza. On set as an artistic director, he delighted in how quickly the stagehands could construct lollipop fields and puffy clouds but kept his contributions specific: He'd painted Katy nude for the album cover and they had a comfortable rapport, so when it came time for a single piece of pink candy floss to be strategically placed on her butt, Will got the nod to set it just so, giving it an artist's touch. Cotton intrinsically understood the intent of the pop caricatures present in Perry's songs. It was what drew him in initially.

"I like to walk this line between something that's kind of ridiculous, but really excellent. And you know, those things can really— that's a thin line," Cotton said. "And I think those guys, Katy Perry and Kesha for that matter, walked that line in just the most entertaining, smart, fun way."

But the line did get blurry. Some of the let-loose impulses of this time, especially considering the fact that many of them were based in fatalistic feelings about the state of the world, were not healthy at all. Dynamics like hookup culture and binge drinking certainly have not gone away, but they felt especially present to me as a young person in high school at this time. There was a line between sleaze and expressiveness that artists playing into the debauchery of this era did not always walk perfectly. But what they ultimately did was give pop stars permission to experiment with style, art, and expressiveness in a way that was no longer "conventionally perfect."

At its best, the pop music of this era embodied self-expression. And no one did that better than Gaga. Yes, her wild outfits and rowdiest songs reflected a certain hedonism, but they also reflected her authentic self. Her elaborate props reflected a genuine interest in art and creativity, and her adoption of onstage drag personas— and outspoken support for LGBTQ+ rights—meaningfully expanded the level of queer representation and iconography that was palatable at the highest levels of pop stardom. On a basic level, her music—and that of her peers who followed her—strengthened the argument that the aughts were playing out as a special decade in pop by dominating the charts and connecting with the social and political feeling of the moment. But it also shaped and strengthened the place of pop music in more lasting ways by stretching the bounds of what's expected from a pop spectacle, making it a lot more than something that's just nice to look at.

11

The End of a Decade

BEFORE WE ADDRESS THE OVERALL IMPACTS OF THE
2000s in pop, we need to define how the decade ended. Just as the
2000s, culturally speaking, really began in 1998 with Britney, they
didn't end neatly on January 1, 2010, but rather a couple years
later, between 2012 and 2013. For the first couple of years of the
(technical) 2010s, the 2000s carried on through the continued
dominance of EDM pop, a still novel fascination with virality, and
post-recession-era indulgences. It was a time of Zac Efron's "YOLO"
tattoo, the self-serve frozen yogurt chain, and a still reputationally
solvent Chris Christie. But that time was coming to an end.

Carly Rae Jepsen is not the artist who ended the 2000s, but she
was the last big star with 2000s vibes to break before the rug was
pulled out from underneath her Golden Goose sneakers. Jepsen is
a mild theater kid from Canada who, in 2007, gained a modicum
of attention for placing third on *Canadian Idol*. The following year,

she put out a folk-pop record called *Tug of War* and began playing shows around Canada with Josh Ramsey, a singer-songwriter and producer best known as the lead vocalist of the pop-rock band Marianas Trench. While on tour they, along with guitarist Tavish Crowe, wrote another folky song based around a four-line refrain. *Hey, she just met you. And this is crazy. But here's her number, so . . .* I think you know the rest. It wasn't even supposed to be the chorus at first. It was Ramsay who recognized that "Call Me Maybe" was a pop song and produced it thus, though the song wasn't even initially slated to be the first single of Jepsen's sophomore album. Somewhat wildly, they didn't hear it as a hit, and Jepsen's manager Jonathan Simkin had to fight for "Call Me Maybe" to be the lead single off *Curiosity*. Released in September, it began a nice trot up the Canadian charts and to garner a bit of international interest.

Enter Justin Bieber, in his bowl cut era.

On December 30, 2011, Bieber tweeted to his fifteen million followers: "Call me maybe by Carly Rae Jepsen is possibly the catchiest song I've ever heard lol." *But was he really loling?* Bieber was serious enough about the song that he lobbied his manager, the now infamous Scooter Braun, to get involved, and Braun quickly signed Jepsen to an international deal on Interscope's Schoolboy label.

In what felt like overnight, the kinetic energy of an undeniable hit and major-label muscle collided to produce arguably the most viral hit of the decade. Not content to let his support stop with a mere tweet, Bieber followed up a month later with a "Call Me Maybe" lip-synch video recorded in his kitchen with then girlfriend Selena Gomez, the members of the boy band Big Time Rush, and Ashley Tisdale. The 2012 of it all is extreme: The video is recorded in the sepia tone of early MacBook Photo Booth filters. Someone has a copy of *The Hunger Games* on hand. Selena pretends to sing into a landline. Everyone, Biebs included, has bangs. Just after the song ends, Bieber finishes the video with a declarative statement, "Swag," and the screen fades to black. The video had more than a million YouTube views in the first twenty-four hours after it went up online (as of this writing, it has over eighty million) and thus, the "Call Me Maybe" lip-synch video was born.

Soon it was a genre unto itself. A group of US Marines made one. The Harvard baseball team did, too. Colin Powell *and* Cookie Monster, who did a parody called "Share It Maybe" about sharing cookies. The guy who produced the Sammy Adams album with "Driving Me Crazy" on it collaborated with a YouTuber going by the username baracksdubs on a video of mashed-up clips of the forty-fourth president of the United States forming the lyrics of "Call Me Maybe." Virality is incorporated into our everyday lives now—we're all making cult vinaigrette dressings and buying skincare products because we saw them shared somewhere—but a decade ago it was intentionally conspicuous. The whole point of flash mobs was for some random place—the DMV, a cafeteria—to suddenly turn absurd, exciting, and shareable. Psy's "Gangnam Style," the other viral hit of 2012, sounded like absolutely nothing else on the *Billboard* charts when it popped. "Call Me Maybe" had all the same memeability, packaged in a once-in-a-decade earworm. The writer Amanda Dobbins, blogging for *Vulture* at the time, put it best: the song was "like [Rebecca Black's] 'Friday,' but good."

Even at the apex of that viral moment, I don't think most observers thought Carly Rae was the future of pop, exactly. I would argue that "Call Me Maybe" is not only good but *great,* but it also does have a certain one-hit-wonder smell to it. But the way she broke out did seem to represent where the industry was going. "Call Me

Maybe" reflected the cheeky, corporate optimism of the late aughts, and it understood social media in the time of the Ice Bucket Challenge and the Ellen DeGeneres selfie. Even if *she* didn't go on to produce more hits, it stood to figure that further hits would happen the way that "Call Me Maybe" had.

But then, they didn't. Carly Rae Jepsen never had another big hit on her own. It wasn't for lack of trying: Schoolboy was so determined to capitalize on the success of "Call Me Maybe" that they rush-released an album, *Kiss,* and signed Jepsen up to collaborate with the electronic pop artist Owl City with the song "Good Time" as its second single. A well-timed summer jam, "Good Time" was a top-ten hit. It peaked at number eight on the *Billboard* Hot 100, you probably sang along to it at a Fourth of July party that year. Jepsen also had an opening slot on Bieber's Believe tour that fall. But *Kiss* didn't sell well, and "Good Time" had a relatively short run on the charts. During the promo for Jepsen's third album, *Emotion*, her team went so far as to recruit Tom Hanks for a music video, but even that didn't create much buzz.

Songs from other artists in the "Call Me Maybe" mold didn't materialize, either. Owl City wound up another artifact of this era, another starry-eyed synth-pop artist who rode an internet moment to his fifteen minutes and then disappeared quickly. (True to her millennial roots, Taylor Swift had an Owl City phase around 2010, and she wrote her song "Enchanted" about meeting Adam Young. That's pretty cool, but if you've ever heard Young's cover of "Enchanted," you know he's unfortunately capable of bungling a moment.) Owl City had a number-one hit with "Fireflies" in 2009, so "Good Time" was useful in the sense that it technically did help both Jepsen and Young pass the one-hit-wonder test, but that was it. Young got no more hugs from no more lightning bugs.

Other pop stars, even those who'd dominated a few years earlier, also faltered. Albums like *Artpop* by Lady Gaga, *Prism* by Katy Perry, and *Animal* by Kesha struggled to capture the zeitgeist as thoroughly as their earlier work had. Jepsen went on to release seven albums of genuinely excellent, if moderately performing, pop music; to sell out arenas; and make some canny choices in collaborators like Ariel Rechtshaid and Dev Hynes, the pop star to indie rock translators of the day. These records allowed her to gradually develop dedicated fan support, critical approval, and a real identity as an artist—the structural underpinnings of pop star success that get lost in the ephemera of an overnight hit, and what she was initially denied. Even so, Interscope eventually gave up on Jepsen as a star in the making. There were no more calls to Oscar winners for favors. "I Really Like You" is her highest-charting song released after 2012; it peaked at number thirty-nine.

So what happened? Theories vary. One is that Jepsen was too old. She was twenty-six when "Call Me Maybe" was released—geriatric in pop star years. Especially in the context of the juvenile vibe of that song, her age became a fixation: horrified sentiments along the lines of *she's like, THIRTY, right?* and *why does she sound like a teenager* were common enough that Jepsen briefly took up vaping while on a recording trip in Sweden because it made her voice sound grittier. Another theory is that Jepsen didn't do the self-mythologizing necessary to build a sense of narrative trajectory. She writes songs about broad feelings, not specific experiences—Carly Rae will never leave her scarf at your sister's house, for example. Have you ever even wondered who she's writing about?

I think what happened is that the era Carly Rae Jepsen broke out in, just after she did, ceased to exist. Just over a year after "Call Me Maybe," on November 22, 2012, a little-known singer-songwriter from New Zealand performing under the name Lorde released an

EP called *The Love Club* on SoundCloud. Alongside it, she released the single "Royals" as a free download. Over lo-fi synths and a sparse beat of finger snaps, her mezzo-soprano critiqued the conspicuous consumption of pop culture writ large.

> *But every song's like 'Gold teeth, Grey Goose, trippin' in the bathroom / Bloodstains, ball gowns, trashing the hotel room,'*

Then within a couple months, the song became the center of the pop-cultural universe she was critiquing. Elevated internationally when Napster cofounder Sean Parker added it to a public Spotify playlist, "Royals" rose, first to the top ranking on the streaming service's viral songs chart and then to the number-one song in America for nine weeks. Lorde released her first studio album, *Pure Heroine,* in September 2013, a brilliant ten tracks of addictively performed boredom. It went triple platinum. She was nominated for four Grammy Awards.

This was something of a conundrum for the musical establishment, the essential problem being that Lorde was making fun of them—and everyone was loving it. A lot of the reaction to Lorde, I think, was rooted in the fact that she made a lot of people feel really old—a lot of critics covering her had the reactionary energy of a midlife crisis. It became a common suggestion that she wasn't actually as young as she claimed, that her sixteen years of age was a marketing ploy designed to wow the press and court teenage fans. "Hi, I'm Ella, and I'm actually forty-five," she deadpanned in a *Vanity Fair* profile. The blog *The Hairpin* once purchased a copy of her birth certificate from the government of New Zealand (DOB: November 7, 1996). "Lorde and Pharrell are the same age and I have the Medieval Tapestry that proves this," Desus Nice tweeted a while back.

This was the fissure that marked the real end of the 2000s in pop—the end of a decade, but the start of an age as some might say. Lorde was critiquing a kind of pop/hip-hop stardom, but she also was a self-professed pop star. She told *The New York Times* that she considered herself "a pop princess at heart," but that "pop is about distilling what you say and making it easy. And the way I write isn't about making things easy," she said. "It's a weird juxtaposition." The juxtaposition with the 2000s was that pop à la Lorde was much smaller and more intimate than it had been. Artists who popped up in Lorde's image in the mid-2010s like Halsey, Alessia Cara, and Daya were characterized in subgenres that emphasized their quiet nature, like sad girl pop and bedroom pop, where hooks took a backseat to *vibes*. Folky groups like Gotye, the Lumineers, and fun. got big. Post Malone was just getting started, and mumbly Sound-Cloud rappers thrived. Even song titles seemed to make themselves chiller and smaller for a lowercase world: "thank u, next," "rockstar," "bad guy," and, eventually, *folklore*. Atop the hip-hop world sat Drake, the vibiest of them all.

The smart analysis, at the time and maybe still, was that this represented a permanent shift in what we listened to, mostly due to changes in technology. Streaming was not fully accepted as the way of the future until Apple moved away from its pay-per-song model in 2015 with the launch of Apple Music, but paid subscription services and on-demand streaming were the fastest-growing revenue categories for the recording industry writ large by 2012. The *sounds* of streaming, too, were all over artist catalogs—shorter songs that could rack up stream counts quickly, chill sounds that worked well on looping playlists. The most critical performance metric became the amount of time someone spent listening to a piece of music, which encouraged artists, labels, and the streamers themselves to cater to audiences who were doing other stuff while they were listening. Playlist names were often defined by what you plan to do

while playing them—"Get Chores Done," "Moody Dinner Party,"
"Pre-Lobotomy Vibes"—instead of what they actually contained.
Entire features of songwriting seemed to disappear: Seven of the
top-ten songs from 2009 followed standard verse-chorus form; by
2019 only three would. Music slowed down again; "Royals" clocks
in at a plodding eighty-five beats per minute, and the DJ Earworm
mash-up in 2013 went from double speed to half speed. ("That was
the first time I was like, I can't just go club," Roseman says.) The
musician and data analyst Chris Dalla Riva spent years listening to
every number-one hit in *Billboard* Hot 100 history from 1958 until
2022 and found a stark demise in the prevalence of key changes.
From the 1960s through the '90s, around a quarter (23 percent) of
all number-one songs featured a key change, but from 2010 to
2020, there was just one number-one song that did so: Drake and
Travis Scott's "Sicko Mode," from 2018. But in many other ways,
"Sicko Mode" is the ultimate streaming song—it follows no traditional structure but stitches three seemingly disconnected parts
into a Frankensteined hit.

Dalla Riva has a couple potential explanations for what happened
to the key change. The first is the rise of hip-hop. Though the most
popular songs that cross over from those genres tend to be the most
melodic, rap is still a genre more interested in rhythm than melody,
and therefore less likely to emphasize something like key structure.
The second is that the digital ways of modern songwriting, where
artists and producers construct music with programs like Pro Tools
that display stacks of musical elements on top of the other, encourage
writers to think "vertically" while making creations instead of "horizontally." Thinking vertically means thinking about one section of a
song at a time—a producer might arrange the baseline, melody, and
harmonies of the verse of a song, then do the same for the chorus,
then the bridge. Thinking horizontally, though, prioritizes how the

song will flow from section to section—a producer might arrange the baseline for the entire song, then do the melody all the way through, then the harmonies. A horizontal production style might encourage more key changes because it's a change that emphasizes how the song progresses. Absolutely none of this favors the big, "Call Me Maybe"–style sing-along. What it does favor are all the Lordes and the Drakes and the Gotyes who thrived in the streaming-era 2010s.

That, to me, was the end of the 2000s in pop music. Sounds shifted away from the big and the bright to the wry and atmospheric. The uniting feature of these shifts was the changes from the previous decade finally setting in—the move to streaming; the growing understanding of the internet, social media, and virality; and the embrace of big-tent pop and new technologies. These changes were born in the 2000s, but once they were baked in, they became subjects of ironic meta-commentary, like Lorde's, instead of gleeful celebration, like Jepsen's. No longer were pop stars partying all night . . . instead they were loitering around or sitting at home, making sardonically snarky comments about the partiers. I'd mark the raucous, EDM-inflected years from 2009 to 2012, which coincided with the peak years of the flash mob and other viral phenomena, as the closing chapter of 2000s pop. After that, trends shifted toward the vibey cool that would undergird a lot of the 2010s. But though the aughts were over, they certainly left a mark.

12

The Start of an Age

THE IDEA OF WRITING A BOOK ABOUT THE POP STARS OF the 2000s came to me for the first time during the summer of 2020, but I didn't write the majority of this book until 2023. During those years, something funny happened. The musical and cultural decade I was so excited to revisit *came back*. The first big sign was Olivia Rodrigo. In 2021, Gen Z's hottest pop star released her triumphant first album, *Sour*, which quickly became the most successful debut album ever released by a female artist in the streaming era. Rodrigo's breakout single was "Driver's License," the piano ballad that introduced her as a singer-songwriter who wrote breakup tunes in her bedroom (yet who deployed notable facility with an F-bomb), and she followed that up with the synth-poppy "Deja Vu." Neither song sounded terribly out of place amid the rest of 2021 pop; "Deja Vu" even spawned a mild controversy given its similarities to Taylor Swift's "Cruel Summer." But it was Rodrigo's third single, "Good 4 U," that placed her in the lineage of mid-aughts pop punk.

It was all there—the crunchy guitars; the chatspeak song title;

the callback to Paramore's "Misery Business," obvious enough for the band to retroactively get a cut of the songwriting royalties— "Good 4 U" hit all the Warped Tour kid erogenous zones. It inspired a TikTok trend about millennial women reviving their inner punks. "Good 4 U" became the biggest song off *Sour*—bigger than "Driver's License"—and its sound, along with similarly bratty tracks "Brutal" and "Jealousy, Jealousy," defined Rodrigo's artistic lane.

There were plenty of other signs of an aughts revival beyond O-Rod. Machine Gun Kelly had a big moment with his own pop-punk record, 2020's *Tickets to My Downfall*. In 2022, the When We Were Young music festival was revived with My Chemical Romance and Paramore as headliners, with Lavigne, 3OH!3, the All-American Rejects, Bright Eyes, and Dashboard Confessional among the supporting acts. David Guetta and Bebe Rexha revived "Blue (Da Ba Dee)" by Eiffel 65, which originally peaked on the Hot 100 in January 2000. In the summer of 2023, the three biggest pieces of pop culture were tours by a thirty-three-year-old Taylor Swift, a forty-one-year-old Beyoncé, and *Barbie,* which capitalized on the story of a doll whose most popular years all came before 2010. Even when a new generation of stars arrived, the Sabrina Carpenters and Chappell Roans all came with nods to the Katys and the Gagas who came before them. The nostalgia was palpable. Butterfly clips started showing up in the gift baggies at the bachelorette parties of my first friends to get married. Consignment platforms like The RealReal promoted edits of "going-out" tops and listings of Fendi baguette bags in *Sex and the City*–era dark denim or bright sequins. Mall retailers like Abercrombie revived themselves and the preferred rise of jeans among the fashionable set fell to hip-bone-exposing lows. *Vogue* was publishing articles about the return of indie sleaze, a viral essay in *The Cut* talked about a vibe shift. Travis Barker from Blink-182 married a Kardashian!

What is it about a trend cycle coming back around that's so satisfying? There's something powerful about seeing or hearing the things that felt important in the impressionable throes of adolescence validated in adulthood. It's a joy simply to relive these sounds and trends and to feel that validation—I'm not even sure if that Bebe Rexha song is "good," per se, and yet I went through the process of resetting my SoundCloud password so that I could listen to it on repeat before Rexha and Guetta got it uploaded on paid streaming services. From a commercial perspective, it's no accident that microgenerational tastes come back in vogue in step with those generations coming of age and gaining disposable income. (Thank you for buying this book, by the way!)

I think what's really most appealing about any nostalgic revival is the chance to revisit a formative era with the knowledge gained by having already lived through it. It's not really about going back in time; as much as it might be important to me that people know how much "Good 4 U" owes to Paramore, it wasn't "Misery Business" that was my top-played song of 2021. It's more fun to listen to the new stuff and compare and contrast—for instance, I'm firmly of the camp that the more slut-shamey moments of "Misery Business"(Hayley Williams calls a girl a whore) are cathartically true to the song's time. It's interesting to note, though, that there's none of that in "Good 4 U." In fact, Rodrigo's biggest kiss-off line references her ex bettering himself for his new girlfriend through seeing a therapist—that Rodrigo found for him. By seeing what a new generation takes from eras past we understand their impact. We revive old styles not just to turn back the clock but to benchmark what has changed in the time since.

That impulse shares a lot in common with the project of this book. In revisiting the stories of these aughties pop stars, we get a sense of what was different about the pop-cultural world they inhabited, and, especially, what's changed since as a result of them. And we understand the hand they had in making those changes happen, often by forcing people to reconsider everything that a pop star could be, and why they deserved to be taken seriously.

Looking at today's pop landscape, the image of modern pop stardom that arises is one that was built in the aughts. To me, it's clearly visible in three main ways. The first has to do with genre. Though hip-hop, in hindsight, has a claim to the nineties, the aughts were the first decade in which the music industry writ large started to move beyond the rock era, which led to more cultural and critical acclaim for pop music. When we revisit the trials and tribulations of Avril Lavigne, we see that shift coming in fits and starts. When we examine Beyoncé's early solo days, we see how she merged music and celebrity so that pop became hip-hop and hip-hop became pop. In 2004, Ashlee Simpson began a poptimist debate that fully sunk in at the end of the decade, when Rihanna, Katy Perry, and Lady Gaga brought electronic music to the center of pop and dealt a blow to the idea, long weaponized against pop, that music that is "manufactured" is inherently lesser.

It's not right to say that pop (or hip-hop) has *replaced* rock as the bedrock genre of the music industry, but it is right to say that genre itself is a more minor concern than it used to be, and that pop is in no way relegated to second-tier status. There is a huge amount of thoughtful attention paid, by critics, media members, and by fans, to the work of pop stars, and this attention generally understands pop stars on their own terms. An artist like Olivia Rodrigo, for instance, doesn't fend off the same queries about "authenticity" that

Lavigne did despite using similar instruments and sounds in her songs, and someone like Chappell Roan can move between pop, rock, and country with ease. Sonically, pop music is increasingly fluid and hard to define—for the last seven years, only 48 percent of what's on the *Billboard* Top 100 year-end survey makes it on the year-end Top 100 for Top 40 radio. And many of the biggest hits of the last several years have blurred genre lines, like Lil Nas X's rhinestone-clad country hit "Old Town Road"; or Bieber, Luis Fonsi, and Daddy Yankee's pop-reggaeton love child, "Despacito," the biggest songs of 2019 and 2017, respectively. These songs and artists are part of a rising trend in global music, but they're also a by-product of a widened understanding of what can be a pop song.

Another space of major change comes in how we relate to pop stars as celebrities. As the experiences of Britney Spears and other stars who were subjected to the peak of the tabloid era have collectively become a subject of national reflection, media outlets are far more restrained in celebrity coverage than they used to be. This is certainly for the best, yet, as this change has coincided with the rise of stan culture online and the replacement of much of traditional media with social media, two countercurrents have emerged. One is that while traditional media is genuinely more thoughtful when it comes to treating public figures as human beings now than it was in the mid-aughts, hundreds of millions outside of the press have been empowered to fill in the gaps. The other is that as social media has heightened the parasociality of our relationships with pop stars and other celebrities—and as stars like Taylor Swift have built those communities into features of modern pop stardom—pop stars have become rooting interests, like sports teams we've chosen through thick and thin rather than raw cultural material.

Technology forms the basis of that change, and, really, it's the bedrock of several of these shifts. Without the spread of the internet, social media, and computer software that influenced producers, many of them wouldn't have happened. And without the rise of MP3s, digital downloads, Napster, and eventually the streaming era, the 2000s in the music industry would have looked wildly different. If there's one theme I was surprised by in terms of how sharply it came through as I was researching and writing this book, it was how much the economic uncertainty of the aughts, particularly in the music industry, showed through in the music itself. One could argue that the demise of the "sellout" was a reflection of the financial pressure artists faced, as was the collapsing space between indie and mainstream pop. Poptimism, too, reflects some need to sell downloads and tickets.

I'm so happy to live in a world where pop music gets the respect it deserves. Where there's rich and varied coverage of pop stars as artists, not just as celebrities. People care about music because it brings them together, which gives the songs and artists that reflect society on a massive stage an essential role. Whether it was Britney Spears provoking a reactionary strain in culture coming out of the nineties, Beyoncé representing the triumph of hip-hop and R&B in music in the highest echelons of celebrity, or Lady Gaga demonstrating the joy and recklessness of life in the wake of the 2008 financial crisis, popular music is a mirror of the world. Thinking along these lines, it seems totally illogical that this music could be dismissed as simple or shallow. But it's not an accident that these stories are women's stories. Through so much of pop history, the genre has been dismissed largely because of its audience—the young women who gravitate to this music, excite in it, and see themselves reflected in it. As a young millennial woman myself, it's gratifying to recognize the fallacy in that, and it is especially satisfying to have lived through—and look back on—a musical decade that eroded that bias. The aughts were a harrowing but magical time in music for women, and it was because of the ways they upended old norms and forged new pathways that the artists who followed them were taken more seriously. A decade, but also—to paraphrase Taylor Swift—the start of an age.

Acknowledgments

This book would simply not exist without Anthony Mattero, the best agent, advocate, and cheerleader I could possibly ask for. Thank you for cold-emailing me, following up, and convincing me I could do this. Thank you, also, for your Dua Lipa takes. To Sydney Collins and Sara Weiss, we figured out this book together and it was an honor and a privilege. Thank you for your brilliance, hard work, patience, and kindness.

To Andy Lefkowitz, Pamela Alders, and Ali Wagner, thank you for helping this book become, well, an actual book. To Ralph Fowler, thank you for the gorgeous design and making my Y2K dreams come to life. To Shasta Clinch, thank you for your eagle-eyed copyedits.

To all my colleagues, editors, producers, and friends at *The Ringer* and *The Boston Globe,* thank you for making me a better writer. Thank you to Bill Simmons for bringing me on and encouraging me to cover Taylor Swift. To Nathan Hubbard, I found my pop-culture-girlie voice with you and I'm forever grateful for it. I love our pod so much. No one has heard me yap about pop stars more than you and kept coming back—thank you.

To Matt James, Jason Lipshutz, Michael Cadoch, Butch Walker, Scott Spock, Guy Zapoleon, Michelle Santosuosso, Will Cotton, and so many others who picked up the phone when I was trying to figure out what this book should be. Thank you for taking that chance and giving me your time and insights.

There is no group of people I'm more grateful for and indebted to than the list of authors and journalists whose work shows up in the bibliography of this book! Thank you for teaching me and feeding a lifelong obsession.

To my parents, I love you. Thank you for raising me around music and writing. To Bobby, we built a life together while I wrote this book, and I've felt your love and support every second. I love you so much and I can't wait to marry you. Thank you for always doing the dishes while I wrote about Kelly Clarkson. To Jocelyne, David, Caitie, Chris, and every DeNunzio, Giroux, and Shaughnessey whose enthusiasm and encouragement is unmissable, I am the absolute luckiest person ever to count you as family.

To my dear friends: Katie, Eliana, Maggie, Tafarii, Anna, Alex, Ed, Pavla, Annie, Tori, Meghan, Bridget, Olivia, Renée, Sammy, Rachel, Chloe, Nicole. You are simply the best people. You've listened to me talk about this book for so long. I love you; I'm so lucky to know you! To those of us who lived through some of the aughts together, I cherish and shudder at the mems. Alex, thank you for cheering me on even when you thought I was writing about German pop stars. Chloe, my author buddy, thank you for likening book-writing to childbirth. That's probably not quite right but it got me through some moments. To James J., thank you for always playing my songs!

Thank you to Taylor Swift! You are really good at your job and you've done an awful lot for me without even knowing it. Last but certainly not least, to everyone who has spent any time at all with this book, or any of my work. It means the world. Thank you for obsessing over pop stars with me.

With love and appreciation,
Nora

Notes

xvii *"move from bubblegum"* Touré, "'N Sync: True Tales of the Pop Life," *Rolling Stone,* August 16, 2001.

3 *"The End of the World"* Richard Lacay, "The End of the World as We Know It," *Time,* January 18, 1999.

5 *"I'm like, 'What is this?'"* Sharon Dastur to author, July 27, 2023.

6 *Zapoleon considers* Guy Zapoleon to author, June 28, 2023.

6 *"heroines"* "South Africa: Prince Charles Meets Mandela and the Spice Girls," *Associated Press,* October 31, 1997.

7 *"I think there's"* Ibid.

10 *In 2020,* **Rolling Stone** "The 100 Greatest Debut Singles of All Time," *Rolling Stone,* May 19, 2020.

12 *"I was expecting"* Steve Dennis, *Britney: Inside the Dream* (New York: HarperCollins, 2009), p. 113.

13 *"Britney was trying"* John Seabrook, *The Song Machine: Inside the Hit Factory* (New York: W. W. Norton, 2015), p. 87.

13 *"Sheryl Crow music, but younger"* Steven Daly, "Britney Spears, Teen Queen," *Rolling Stone,* April 15, 1999.

13 *"Because I can dance to it"* Ibid.

14 *"She said"* Seabrook, p. 89.

15 *"I arrived at the studio"* Radio Sweden, *The Cheiron Saga,* 2008.

17 *"I grew up on"* Neil McCormick, "Max Martin interview: the pop maestro on making Shakespeare sound like Taylor Swift and Britney Spears," *The Telegraph,* November 16, 2019.

19 *"'I am not going to sing'"* Nolan Feeney, "Ariana Grande Is Fully Aware That the Lyrics of 'Break Free' Make No Sense," *Time,* August 7, 2014.

19 *"I was like"* Cory Midgarden, "Why TLC Said 'Hell No' To Britney's '. . . Baby One More Time,'" *MTV.com,* October 17, 2013.

20 *"All those chords"* Seabrook, p. 90.

20 *"Holy shit"* Ibid., 91.

21 *"What a sexy song"* Daly, "Britney Spears, Teen Queen."

22 *"The outfits looked"* Britney Spears to *People* magazine, 2000. This interview is not accessible online but this quote has been preserved in news coverage.

23 *In April 1999* Daly, "Britney Spears, Teen Queen."

26 *"Raunchy," "explicit," and "open-mouth"* Bill Hoffmann, "Madonna's 2 Kinky Kisses—Smooches with Britney and Christina," *New York Post,* August 29, 2003.

26 *"I don't know if"* *The Oprah Winfrey Show,* "Season 18, Episode 127," September 16, 2003.

35 *"The music I was making"* Brittany Spanos, "Christina Aguilera Shares How Heartbreak, Vulnerability, 'Stupid Tabloids,' and a Teen Crush on Dave Navarro Shaped Her Most Daring Album," *Rolling Stone,* October 22, 2022.

36 *"It made me sad"* Ibid.

38 *"A primer"* "The 50 Most Important Recordings Of The Decade: S-Z," *NPR,* November 16, 2009.

41 *"Hey, um, okay"* Carson Daly interview with Avril Lavigne, *Total Request Live,* MTV, aired May 30, 2002.

42 *"Britney and Christina Aguilera"* Mickey McMonagle, "Avril's Biting Back," *The Sunday Mail,* May 9, 2004.

42 *"Most girls were"* Ibid.

45 *"Ciao, Britney!"* Chris Willman, "Avril Lavigne The Anti-Britney," *Entertainment Weekly,* November 1, 2002.

46 *"a Mandy Moore kind of movie"* *The Townsville Bulletin,* May 2007.

46 *"Avril doesn't really dance"* Britney Spears to *W* magazine, 2003. This interview is not accessible online but this quote has been preserved in news coverage.

47 *"I created punk"* *Seventeen* magazine, 2002.

50 *Reid called* Scott Spock to author, June 26, 2023.

51 *"It's got to go"* Ibid.

52 *"Songwriting is"* Jenny Eliscu, "Avril Lavigne: Little Miss Can't Be Wrong," *Rolling Stone,* March 20, 2003.

53 *"She was singing along"* Spock, June 26, 2023.

53 *Spock says* Ibid.

54 *"I just thought"* Butch Walker to author, July 18, 2023.

55 *"I don't get it"* Ibid.

55 *"We would play her T-Rex"* Ibid.

56 *Even a positive* Kelefa Sanneh, "Under My Skin," *Rolling Stone,* June 10, 2004.

56 *"the music is so anodyne"* Alexis Petridis, "Avril Lavigne, Under My Skin," *The Guardian,* May 20, 2004.

58 *"You may have heard"* Avril Lavigne's Myspace blog post has been taken down, but the text has been preserved in news coverage.

58 *"Some of the songs"* Ibid.

61 *"It's just a dumb internet rumor"* Ilana Kaplan, "Avril Lavigne on *Head Above Water,* near-death experiences, and that crazy conspiracy theory," *Entertainment Weekly,* February 11, 2019.

61 *"The blog was a way"* The AvrilEstaMorta Facebook page has been deactivated, but the text has been preserved on the original blog page.

66 *He was getting* Spock, June 26, 2023.

67 *"Not only will Ms. Phair"* Meghan O'Rourke, "Liz Phair's Exile in Avril-ville," *The New York Times,* June 22, 2003.

68 *A week after the* SNL *incident* Kelefa Sanneh, "The Rap Against Rockism," *The New York Times,* October 31, 2004.

69 *"Countless critics assail"* Ibid.

70 *In 2006* Katharine Q. Seelye, "Ashlee's Nose Job Is Last Straw for New Editor of Marie Claire," *The New York Times,* July 31, 2006.

70 *"She was quoting"* Ibid.

73 *"becoming worshipful"* Chris Richards, "Do you want Poptimism? Or do you want the truth?" *The Washington Post,* April 17, 2015.

78 *"the single most"* Mauch Matthias, Robert M. MacCallum, Mark Levy, and Armand M. Leroi, "The evolution of popular music: USA 1960–2010," *Royal Society Open Science* 2, no. 5 (2015).

81 *a 2017 study*   Tori Owens, "As America grows more diverse, fashion magazine covers are slow to show progress," *Peninsula Press,* August 25, 2017.

82 *"I remember Clive"*   Michelle Santosuosso to author, July 21, 2023.

86 *"I love the idea"*   Joe D'Angelo, "Road to the Grammys: The Making of Beyoncé's 'Crazy In Love,' " *MTV News,* February 4, 2004.

90 *On the podcast*   Jill Hopkins and Joe DeCeault, hosts, *Making Beyoncé,* "Beyoncé BONUS: Fearlessly Herself," WBEZ Chicago, March 6, 2020.

95 *"exists solely in the fevered imaginations"*   Nathan Rabin, "The Bataan Death March of Whimsy Case File #1: *Elizabethtown,*" *The A.V. Club,* January 25, 2007.

101 *Lorde brought that up*   Jonah Weiner, "The Return of Lorde," *The New York Times Magazine,* April 12, 2017.

101 *"If they would just"*   Chris Willman, "Dr. Luke: The Billboard Cover Story," *Billboard,* September 3, 2010.

103 *"They weren't prepared"*   Ibid.

104 *"poisonous varmint"*   Rob Sheffield, "Yeah Yeah Yeahs: Taking Their Glorious Freak Rock Global," *Rolling Stone,* April 20, 2006.

105 *she hadn't wanted to sing*   Clive Davis with Anthony DeCurtis, *The Soundtrack of My Life* (New York: Simon & Schuster, 2013), p. 507.

105 *"Let's give some backstory"*   Kelly Clarkson interview, *Watch What Happens Live with Andy Cohen,* "Season 20, Episode 111," Bravo, June 27, 2023.

106 *In his memoir*   Davis with DeCurtis, pps. 507–516.

106 *"I cried because he hated it"*   Seabrook, p. 142.

110 *"Bimbo Summit"*   Maureen Callahan, "3 Bimbos of the Apocalypse—No Clue, No Cares, No Underwear: Meet the Party Posse of the Year," *The New York Post,* November 29, 2006.

112 *"Busted! Fast Food Fiends"*   *Us Weekly* staff, "Stars—They're Just Like US," *Us Weekly,* April 1, 2002.

113 *"The nightclubs of LA"*   Nicole Richie, *The Truth About Diamonds* (New York: Regan Books, 2006), p. 3.

116 *"I would never get"*   George Rush and Joanna Molloy, "When The O.C. Imitates Life," *New York Daily News,* May 20, 2004.

116 *"Celebrity is the enemy"* Lynn Hirschberg, "A Film of One's Own," *The New York Times Magazine,* September 3, 2006.

117 *"somewhere along the lines"* Corey Moss, "Lindsay Bizkit? Lohan Solo Album Combines 'Hip-Hop and Rock,'" *MTV News,* April 21, 2004.

121 *"She's doing her thing"* Jennifer Vineyard, "Scott Storch Says He and Paris Are Making 'Amazing' Music," *MTV News,* August 31, 2005.

122 *"wasn't truly awful"* Randy Lewis, "Formula for Hilton is Simplicity Itself," *Los Angeles Times,* August 22, 2006.

122 *"often both inane and vaguely porny"* Leah Greenblatt, "Paris," *Entertainment Weekly,* August 28, 2006.

130 *"'Rumors' is one"* Naomi McPherson, interview with *Pitchfork* (@pitchfork), TikTok, June 28, 2023.

134 *"Radio does research"* Chris Willman, "Taylor Swift's Road to Fame," *Entertainment Weekly,* February 5, 2008.

135 *"We were able"* Ibid.

136 *"I'm a junior"* Ken Tucker, "CMT Awards meet the Myspace generation," *Reuters,* August 9, 2007.

141 *"young women"* Nancy Kaplan and Eva Farrell, "Weavers of Webs: A Portrait of Young Women on the Net," *The Arachnet Electronic Journal on Visual Culture 2,* no. 3 (1994).

142 *"to maintain connection"* Ibid.

147 *"There was a lot"* Gil Kaufman, "2009 VMAs Oral History: What You Didn't See When Kanye West Rushed the Stage on Taylor Swift," *Billboard,* August 21, 2019.

148 *"The Kanye incident"* Christopher John Farley, "Did the Kanye West Incident Help Taylor Swift's Career?" *Wall Street Journal,* October 23, 2010.

148 *"blowing local Tennessee DJs"* Drew Magary, "The Hater's Guide to Taylor Swift," *Deadspin,* November 29, 2010.

158 *"She's Madonna"* Seabrook, p. 186.

158 *"I feel bad about that"* Daniel Kilkelly, "Rihanna 'feels bad' about UK weather," *Digital Spy,* August 23, 2007.

160 *"fucked up music"* T-Pain interview, *This Is Pop,* season 1, episode 1, March 6, 2021.

162   *the average tempo*   Nate Sloan and Charlie Harding, *Switched on Pop: How Popular Music Works, and Why it Matters* (New York: Oxford University Press, 2020), p. 11.

164   *The '07 mix*   Jordan Roseman to author, July 26, 2023.

174   *When Def Jam*   Links to Gaga's early blog posts are no longer live, but the poem "I Do" has been saved on her fan Wiki, Gagapedia.

179   *"She had the art"*   Butch Walker to author, July 18, 2023.

179   *"I was like"*   Ibid.

182   *"I'm trying to"*   Jon Carimanica, "Changing the Face (and Sound) of Rap," *The New York Times,* December 23, 2009.

185   *"I noticed she"*   Will Cotton to author, June 29, 2023.

186   *"I like to"*   Ibid.

190   *"like [Rebecca Black's] 'Friday,' but good"*   Amanda Dobbins interview with Jason Lipshutz, "Carly Rae Jepsen: The Billboard Cover Story," *Billboard,* June 25, 2012.

193   *"Hi, I'm Ella"*   Julie Miller, "Lorde Reveals Her Grammys Date and Her Secret Actual Age," *Vanity Fair,* January 24, 2014.

193   *"Lorde and Pharrell"*   Desus Nice (@desusnice), "Lorde and Pharrell are the same age and I have the Medieval Tapestry that proves this," Twitter (now X), January 27, 2014.

194   *"a pop princess at heart"*   Jon Pareles, "Lorde's 'Royals' Is Class-Conscious," *The New York Times,* December 26, 2013.

195   *"That was the first time"*   Roseman to author, July 26, 2023.

195   *Stark demise*   Chris Dalla Riva, "The Death of the Key Change," *Tedium,* November 9, 2022.

ABOUT THE AUTHOR

NORA PRINCIOTTI is an author and staff writer at *The Ringer* where she covers culture, from Taylor Swift to the National Football League. She also hosts the pop music podcast *Every Single Album*. She was previously a reporter for *The Boston Globe* covering the New England Patriots dynasty. She lives in New York City.

ABOUT THE TYPE

This book was set in Garamond, a typeface originally designed by the Parisian type cutter Claude Garamond (c. 1500–61). This version of Garamond was modeled on a 1592 specimen sheet from the Egenolff-Berner foundry, which was produced from types assumed to have been brought to Frankfurt by the punch cutter Jacques Sabon (c. 1520–80).

Claude Garamond's distinguished romans and italics first appeared in *Opera Ciceronis* in 1543–44. The Garamond types are clear, open, and elegant.